William Shakespeare, Frederick James Furnivall

The Whole Contention (1619)

Part I.

William Shakespeare, Frederick James Furnivall

The Whole Contention (1619)
Part I.

ISBN/EAN: 9783337138783

Printed in Europe, USA, Canada, Australia, Japan

Cover: Foto ©Thomas Meinert / pixelio.de

More available books at **www.hansebooks.com**

THE WHOLE CONTENTION

(1619).

PART I.

THE FIRST PART OF THE CONTENTION OF THE TWO
FAMOUS HOUSES OF YORK AND LANCASTER, WITH THE
DEATH OF THE GOOD DUKE HUMFREY.

THE THIRD QUARTO,

1619.

(Q₁ HAVING BEEN REVIZED BY SHAKSPERE, MARLOWE, AND GREENE
INTO *"THE SECOND PART OF HENRY THE SIXT.")*

A FACSIMILE, BY PHOTOLITHOGRAPHY

(FROM THE BRITISH MUSEUM COPY, C. 34, k. 38),

BY

CHARLES PRAETORIUS.

WITH FOREWORDS BY

FREDERICK J. FURNIVALL,

M.A. TRIN. HALL, CAMBRIDGE; HON. DR. PHIL. BERLIN.

LONDON :
PRODUCED BY C. PRAETORIUS, 14 CLAREVILLE GROVE,
HEREFORD SQUARE, S.W.

1886.

CONTENTS OF FOREWORDS.

40 SHAKSPERE QUARTO FACSIMILES,

ISSUED UNDER THE SUPERINTENDENCE OF DR F. J. FURNIVALL.

1. *Those by W. Griggs.*

No.
1. Hamlet. 1603.
2. Hamlet. 1604.
3. Midsummer Night's Dream. 1600. (Fisher.)
4. Midsummer Night's Dream. 1600. (Roberts.)
5. Loves Labor's Lost. 1598.
6. Merry Wives. 1602.
7. Merchant of Venice. 1600. (Roberts.)
8. Henry IV. 1st Part. 1598.

No.
9. Henry IV. 2nd Part. 1600.
10. Passionate Pilgrim. 1599.
11. Richard III. 1597.
12. Venus and Adonis. 1593.
13. Troilus and Cressida. 1609. (*printing.*)
14. Much Ado About Nothing. 1600. (*fotograft.*)
15. Taming of a Shrew. 1594. (*not yet done.*)

2. *Those by C. Praetorius.*

16. Richard II. 1597. Duke of Devonshire's copy. (*fotograft.*)
17. Merchant of Venice. 1600. (I. R. for Heyes.) (*fotograft.*)
18. Richard II. 1597. Mr Huth. (*fotograft.*)
19. Richard II. 1608. Brit. Mus. (*fotograft.*)
20. Richard II. 1634. (*fotograft.*)
21. Pericles. 1609. Q1.
22. Pericles. 1609. Q2.
23. The Whole Contention. 1619. Part I. (for 2 Henry VI.).
24. The Whole Contention. 1619. Part II. (for 3 Henry VI.).
25. Romeo and Juliet. 1597.
26. Romeo and Juliet. 1599.

27. Henry V. 1600. (*printing.*)
28. Henry V. 1608. (*printing.*)
29. Titus Andronicus. 1600.
30. Sonnets and Lover's Complaint. 1609.
31. Othello. 1622.
32. Othello. 1630.
33. King Lear. 1608. Q1. (N. Butter, *Pide Bull.*)
34. King Lear. 1608. Q2. (N. Butter.)
35. Lucrece. 1594.
36. Romeo and Juliet. Undated. (*fotograft.*)
37. Contention. 1594. (*not yet done.*)
38. True Tragedy. 1595. (*not yet done.*)
39. The Famous Victories. 1598. (*not yet done.*)
40. The Troublesome Raigne. 1591. (For King John : *not yet done.*)

FOREWORDS TO "THE WHOLE CONTENTION,"
1619.

§ 1. THE reason for the appearance of this Third Quarto, *The Whole Contention*, 1619, before the first Quartos of *The Contention* 1594, and *The True Tragedy* 1595, is, that the unique originals of the first Quartos are in the Bodleian, while Mr Praetorius works in the British Museum (where a copy of Q3 is), and the Bodleian authorities refuzed to send their Quartos to be fotograft in the Museum. Next month, however, either Mr Praetorius or his partner will go up to Oxford, and fotograf the 1594 *Contention*, and the 1595 *True Tragedy*, 'in situ'; and their Facsimiles will come to our Subscribers in due course.

'The *Whole* Contention' is, as its name indicates, in one volume, yet its Facsimile appears in two Parts. The reason is, that Mr Quaritch didn't like to double the price of one volume of the Series, while on the other hand Mr Praetorius couldn't afford to give two Parts or volumes as one. To any Subscriber who looks at the necessary cost of the production of these Facsimiles, it must be plain, that, tho' we Editors all work for nothing, 3*s.* a volume can hardly do more than cover the expense of fotografing, lithografing, number-writing, correcting and printing the text, and paying the Printer's bill for the Forewords or Introduction. As Mr Quaritch pays for the 500 copies of every volume on their delivery, and takes his chance of the Series being completed, and the books then selling in sets, he having to incur fresh cost to supply the numbers short through Mr Griggs's fire, no one can deny that he is entitled to such profit on the venture as he may be able to get. The production of the Quartos has turnd solely on his willingness to advance their cost, on delivery. And when any student contrasts the present Series with the hand-made ones by Mr Ashbee, sold by Halliwell at Five Guineas a-piece,—without any helpful Forewords, side-numbers, and marks of differences from the Folio, &c.—he can estimate what he owes to Mr Quaritch, Mr Griggs, Mr Praetorius, and the volunteer Editors, to whom is due the existence of this Series, this great boon to the real student of Shakspere's text.

§ 2. Had the First Quartos of the *Contention* and *True Tragedy* been facsimiled first, the side-marks to this *Whole Contention* of 1619 would have noted only its differences from the First Quartos. But as Q3 was to come out first,—in October last, as I thought, when I markt it in August at Castleton village, on the edge of the

North-Riding moors, 15 miles West of Whitby,—I rezolvd to take the further trouble of marking Q3 by the Folio—or rather, the Globe Shakspere—as well as by Q1.[1] Accordingly the marks on the outer edges of the pages[2] show when Q3 differs from the Globe text (that is, the Folio with a few changes), while the few marks on the inner edges show where Q3 differs from Q1. ' § ' marks lines special to Q3 ; a dot '. ' lines partly alterd from Q1.

§ 3. The main changes which Q3 makes in the text of Q1, showing that some Editor or Reviser workt at it, are four in number, which I arrange here, beside the further revision in the First Folio, as I did in *The New Shakspere Society's Transactions*, 1875-6, p. 285-8. The words in which both Q3 and F1 differ from Q1 are printed in *italics*. The differences special to Q3 are in **clarendon** ; those special to F1 are in SMALL CAPITALS :

I.

1 *Cont.* 1594, 1600, I. ii.	1619. *Cont.* I. ii. (p. 8 below)	1623. 2 *Hen. VI*, I. ii. 25—30.
This night vvhen I was laid in bed, I dreampt that	This night when I was laid in bed, I dreamt	
This my staffe, mine Office badge in Court,	That this my staffe, mine Office badge in Court,	METHOUGHT this staff, mine office-badge in court,
Was broke in two, and on the ends were plac'd	Was broke in *twaine, by whom I* **cannot gesse**:	Was broke in *twain ; by whom I* HAVE FORGOT,
	But as I thinke by the Cardinall. What it bodes	*But, as I think,* IT WAS *by the cardinal,*
	God knowes ; and on the ends were plac'd	And on the PIECES OF THE BROKEN WAND
The heads of the Cardinall of VVinchester,	The heads of *Edmund Duke of Somerset,*	Were plac'd the heads of *Edmund duke of Somerset,*
And William de la Poule first duke of Suffolke.	And William de la Pole, first duke of Suffolke.	And William de la Poole, first duke of Suffolk, THIS WAS MY DREAM : *what it* DOTH *bode, God knows.*

Who is responsible for the italic and clarendon parts of the 1619 edition ? who for the small-capitals part of the 1623 ?

II.

Again, in Act I, scene ii, Q1, 1594 has these two lines :

But ere it be long, Ile go before them all,
Despight of all that seeke to crosse me thus,

---

[1] I forgot to write the Scene- and line-nos. of the Qo. on the inner edge, and afterwards thought it not fair to the lithografer to make him put them in from a corrected proof.

[2] A star * marks the lines not in F1, '†' those alterd in F1. ' < ' marks an omission in Q3 as compared with F1.

In the Quarto of 1619 and the Folio of 1623, are instead,

1619. *Contention*, Act I. sc. ii. l. 61-7 (p. 9 below).	1623. 2 *Henry VI*, Act I. sc. ii. l. 61-7.
Ile **come after you, for** *I cannot* go before,	FOLLOW I MUST : *I cannot* go before,
As long as *Gloster beares this base and humble minde :*	WHILE *Gloster bears this base and humble mind :*
Were I a man, and **Protector as he is,**	*Were I a man,* A DUKE, *and* NEXT OF BLOOD,
Ide **reach to th' crowne, or make some hop** *headlesse :*	*I* WOULD REMOVE THESE TEDIOUS STUMBLING-BLOCKS, AND SMOOTH MY WAY UPON THEIR *headless* NECKS :
And being **but** *a woman, ile not* [*be*] **behinde**	*And, being a woman, I* WILL *not be* SLACK
For *playing of my part, in* spite of all that seek to crosse me thus.	TO *play my part in* FORTUNE'S PAGEANT.

III.

Further again, compare :

1594. *Contention*, p. 19.	1619. 1 *Contention* (p. 18, below).	1623. 2 *Henry VI*, II. i. · 12—14, p. 125.
He knowes his maister loues to be aloft.	*They* know *their* master **sores** a Faulcons pitch.	They know their Master loues to be aloft, AND BEARES HIS THOUGHTS ABOVE HIS Faulcons Pitch.
Humphrey. Faith my . Lord, it is but a base minde	*Hum.* Faith, my lord, it's but a base minde,	*Glost.* My Lord, 'tis but a base IGNOBLE minde,
That can sore no higher than a Falkons pitch.	That sores no higher then *a bird can sore.*	That MOUNTS no higher than a *Bird can sore.*

IV.

Lastly, see these changes :—

1594. *Contention*, p. 25.	1619. 1 *Contention.* (below, p. 23.)	1623. 1st Folio, p. 127-8, 2 *Hen. VI*, II. ii. 12-52.
The second ¹vvas Edmund of Langly,² Duke of Yorke. [see *fift* in Q3, 1619, below.]	The second was *William of Hatfield,* **Who** *dyed* **young.**	The second *William of Hatfield ;* AND the third,
The third vvas Lyonell Duke of Clarence.	The third was Lyonell Duke of Clarence.	Lionel, Duke of Clarence ; NEXT TO WHOM,
The fourth vvas Iohn of Gaunt, The Duke of Lancaster.	The fourth was Iohn of Gaunt, The Duke of Lancaster.	Was Iohn of Gaunt, the Duke of Lancaster ;
The fifth vvas Roger Mortemor, Earle of March.	The fift was * Edmund of Langley, Duke of Yorke.*	The fift, was Edmond Langley, Duke of Yorke ;
The sixt vvas sir Thomas of Woodstocke.	The sixt was William of Windsore, **Who** *dyed* **young.**	The sixt, was Thomas of Woodstock, *Duke of* GLOSTER ;

---

¹ Mr Halliwell prints *w* for *vv* of the original. ² Both mistakes.

1594. *Contention*, p. 25.

William of Winsore vvas the seuenth and last.

Novv, Edvvard the blacke Prince he died before his father, and left / behinde him Richard, that aftervvards vvas King, Crovvnde by / the name of Richard the second, and he died vvithout an heire. /

* Edmund of Langly Duke of Yorke * died, and left behind him tvvo / daughters, Anne and Elinor. / Lyonell Duke of Clarence died, and left behinde Alice, Anne, / and Elinor, that vvas after married to my father, and by her I / claime the Crovvne,

as the true heire to Lyonell Duke / of Clarence, the third sonne to Edward the third. Now sir. In the / time of Richards raigne, Henry of Bullingbrooke, sonne and heire / to Iohn of Gaunt, the Duke of Lancaster fourth sonne to Edward / the third, he claimde the Crowne, deposde the Merthfull King, and / as both you know, in Pomphret Castle harmelesse Richard was / shamefully murthered, and so by Richard's death came the house of / Lancaster vnto the Crowne. /
Sals. Sauing your tale my

1619. 1 *Content'on.*
(below, p. 23.)

The seauenth and last was Sir Thomas of Woodstocke, *Duke of Yorke.*

Now Edward the blacke prince dyed before his Father, leauing behinde him **two sonnes**; **Edward, borne at Angolesme,**[1] **who died young, and** Richard, that was after crowned king by the name of Richard the second, who dyed without an heyre.

Lyonell duke of Clarence dyed, and left him **one only** *daughter,* **named**† *Phillip, who* **was** *married* **to** *Edmund Mortimer, earle* / *of March,*† **and Vlster**: and so by her I claime the Crowne [&c. as in Q1, 1594].

1623. 1st Folio, p. 127-8,
2 Hen. VI, II. ii. 12-52.

William of Windsor was the seuenth, and last.

Edward the Black-Prince dyed before his Father, And left behinde him Richard, HIS ONELY SONNE, WHO after EDWARD THE THIRD'S DEATH, RAIGN'D AS King, TILL Henry Bullingbrooke, Duke of Lancaster, THE ELDEST Sonne and Heire OF Iohn of Gaunt, CROWN'D BY THE NAME OF HENRY THE FOURTH, SEIZ'D ON THE REALME, depos'd the RIGHTFULL King, SENT HIS POORE QUEENE TO FRANCE, FROM WHENCE SHE CAME,

And HIM to Pumfret; WHERE, as ALL you know,
Harmelesse Richard was murthered TRAITEROUSLY.
Warw. FATHER, THE DUKE HATH TOLD THE TRUTH;
THUS GOT the House of Lancaster the Crowne.
Yorke. WHICH NOW THEY HOLD BY FORCE, AND NOT BY RIGHT;
FOR RICHARD, THE FIRST SONNES HEIRE, BEING DEAD,
THE ISSUE OF THE NEXT SONNE SHOULD HAUE REIGN'D.
Salisb. BUT WILLIAM OF HATFIELD *dyed* WITHOUT AN HEIRE.
Yorke. THE THIRD SONNE, Duke of Clarence, FROM WHOSE LINE I clayme the Crowne,
HAD ISSUE *Phillip,*† *a Daughter,*
Who marryed Edmond Mortimer, Earle of March :†

---

[1] 'In the nine and thirtith yéere of king Edwards reigne [1365], and in the moneth of Februarie, in the citie of Angolesme, was borne the first sonne of prince Edward, and was named after his father, but he departed this life the seuenth yeare of his age.'—*Holinshed,* ed. 2, vol. iii. p. 397, col. 1, ll. 56—61.

The reuiser of the 1619 *Contention* must have taken some pains with his genealogy.—W. G. STONE.

1594. *Contention*, p. 25.
Lord, as I haue heard, in the raigne / of Bullen-brooke, the Duke of Yorke did claime the Crowne, and / but for Owin Glendor, had bene King./

Yorke. True. But so it for-tuned then, by meanes of that mon/strous rebel Glendor, the noble Duke of York was done to death, / and so euer since the heires of Iohn of Gaunt haue possessed the Crowne.

But if the issue of the elder should sucseed before the is/sue of the yonger, then am I lawfull heire vnto the kingdome./ [1]

1623. 1st Folio, p. 127-8, 2 *Hen. VI*, II. ii. 12-52.
EDMOND IIAD ISSUE, ROGER, EARLE OF MARCII;
ROGER IIAD ISSUE, EDMOND, ANNE, AND ELI-ANOR.
Salisb. THIS EDMOND, in the Reigne of Bulling-brooke,
AS I HAUE READ, LAYD clayme VNTO the Crowne,
And but for Owen Glendour, had beene King;
WHO KEPT HIM IN CAPTIUITIE, TILL IIE DYED.
BUT, TO THE REST.
Yorke. IIIS ELDEST SISTER, ANNE,
MY MOTHER, BEING IIEIRE VNTO THE CROWNE,
MARRYED RICHARD, EARLE OF CAMBRIDGE,
WHO WAS TO EDMOND LANGLEY,
EDWARD THE THIRDS FIFT SONNES SONNE;
BY IIER I CLAYME THE KINGDOME:
SHE WAS IIEIRE TO ROGER, EARLE OF MARCH,
WHO WAS TIIE SONNE OF EDMOND MORTIMER,
WHO MARRYED PIIILLIP, SOLE DAUGIITER
VNTO LIONEL, DUKE OF CLARENCE.
So, if the Issue of the elder SONNE
Succeed before the younger, I am KING.

§ 4. The chief of the smaller changes[2]—some of which are mistakes, others due to a Reviser,—are as follows :—

	Q3	Q1	F1
p. 3, l. 8	twenty	then the	twenty
p. 4, l. 49	thirty day	30.	thirtieth
,, l. 50	Dutcheſſe	Dutches	Dutcheſſe
,, l. 52	fa———	fa.	father.
,, l. 56	ore	ouer	[not in]
p. 5, top line,	My Lord of Yorke, I pray do	Vnckle of *Winchef-ter*, I pray	as in Q1.
,, l. 57	*Yorke*	Cardinall	*Win.*
,, l. 57-8	Dutcheſſe	Duches	Dutcheſſe
,, l. 71	for all	all, for	all for
,, l. 93	ſpent quite	ſpent	[not in]
,, l. 110	Dutcheſſe	Dutches	Dutchy
p. 6, l. 137	Lords	Lord	Lord

[1] The genealogy in the 1594 edition of *Contention* is so inaccurate that I should doubt the existence of any historical work from which it could be derived. The reviser of the edition published in 1619 would find in Holinshed (edition 2, vol. iii. pp. 657-9) the articles of agreement between IIenry VI. and Richard Duke of York, whereby IIenry VI. was to be acknowledged as King during his life, and the Duke was declared to be heir apparent.
In this document there is a genealogy (p. 657), starting from IIenry III, which gives Edward III.'s sons and Richard Duke of York's descent from Lionel Duke of Clarence. Henry VI.'s descent from John of Gaunt is also compared with Mortimer's line (p. 657-8).—W. G. STONE.
[2] Changes of 'and' to '&', and vice versâ, and different stops, abbreviations, and spellings (*Hum.* Q3, *Humphr.* Q1 ; S. Q3, Saint Q1), or separations or join-ings of words (Me thought, Methought ; be gone, begone ; &c.), are not notist.

	Q3	Q1	F1
p. 6, l. 148	you well	well you	[*not in*]
,, l. 186	of the	of	o' th'
p. 8, l. 254	grapple	graffle	grapple
,, l. 26	(Q3) (*See abuv, No. I,* p. iv.)		
p. 9, l. 34	the	th'	[*not in*]
,, St. Dir.	*Enter a*	Enters a	*Enter*
,, l. 59	vs	vs vs	vs
,, l. 62-6	(Q3) (*See abuv, No. II,* p. iv-v.)		
p. 10, l. 76	*Rye*	*Ely*	[*not in*]
,, l. 86	they may	they may	[,,]
p. 11, l. 30	to	vnto	to
,, l. 36	Who's	Whose	Who is
p. 12, l. 23	what's	what	What's
,, l. 26	me	me, me	[*not in*]
,, l. 78	to speake	nor speake	[,,]
,, l. 82	take her for	takes her for the	take her for the
,, l. 83	She beares a Dukes whole reuennewes on her backe.	[*not in*]	She beares a Dukes Reuenues on her backe
,, l. 69	into	to	to
p. 13, st. dir.	*Then entereth*	and enter	*Enter*
,, l. 108	thinkes	thinke	[*not in*]
,, l. 115	best	the best	the best
,, l. 123	ore	ouer	of
,, l. 125	a King	King	King
p. 14, l. 190	worship	Maiestie	Maiestie
,, l. 200	master	my Lord	my Lord
,, l. 205	worship	Maiestie	Maiestie
,, l. 212-13	[*line out*]	Which shall be on the thirtith of this month	[*not in*]
p. 15, l. 217	to	for to	[,,]
,, l. 151, &c.	wert	wart	[,,]
,, l. 209	ore	ouer	in
,, l. 213	right	rights	[,,
p. 17, l. 35	awaites	awayt	await
p. 18, l. 10	do	done	doe
,, l. 11-14	(*See abuv, No. III,* p. v.)		
,, l. 25-6	do't	doate	doe it
,, l. 29	t'like	it like	't like
p. 19, l. 39*	thee	rhee	[*not in*]
,, l. 51	Gods mother	Faith	by Gods Mother
,, l. 64	at the	at his	[*not in*]
,, l. 82	[prefix *om.*]	*Humphrey*	*King*
,, l. 83	please you Maiesty	sir,	an't like your Grace
p. 20, l. 95	are	are thou	art thou
,, l. 97	off	off on	off of
,, l. 110	Red	Why red	Red
p. 21, *St. Dir.*	ierke	girke	[*not in*]
p. 23, l. 12, to p. 24, l. 50	(*See No. IV, abuv,* p. v-vii).		
p. 24, l. 34	third	the third	[,,]

	Q3	Q1	F1
p. 24, l. 21	in	In the	[*not in*]
,, l. 43	putte	done	[,,]
,, l. 53	proceedings	plaine proceedings	plaine proceedings
p. 25, l. 4	State	States	[*not in*]
,, l. 11	crime	crimes	[,,]
p. 26, l. 27	this my	my	[,,]
,, l. 68	affraid	affeard	afraid
p. 27, 1 *St. Dir. Peter*		and Peter	*and Peter*
p. 28, l. 20	doft	doeft	do'ft
p. 29, l. 49	ore	ouer	ouer
,, l. 55	canft	can	canft
,, l. 72	— — —	sodeine	clofe dealing
,, l. 85	not me	me not	me not
p. 30, *St. Dir.*	Buckingham,	Buckingham, and	Buckingham
,, l. 9	the	that	that
,, l. 15	Yet	And	[*not in*]
,, l. 28	[*not in*]	And with long life,	[,,]
		Iesus preferue his grace,	
	Honouring	Honouring	[,,]
,, l. 36	call't	call it	call it
p. 31, l. 103	I am	am I	am I
,, l. 106	Through	By	By meanes
,, l. 110	me helpe	helpe me	helpe me
p. 32, l. 170	be	be well	be well
p. 34, l. 288	And burnes and fpoiles the Country as they go	[*put after* l. 291' *in* Q1]	[*not in*]
,, l. 290	good	very good	[,,]
,, l. 318	fortunes 'gainft	fortune againft	[,,]
,, l. 328	Ile	I wil	I
p. 35, l. (373)	(For he is like him euery kinde of way)	[*not in*]	[*not in*]
p. 36, l. 20	'gainft	againft	'gainft
,, l. 29	of Glofters	Glofter is	Glofter is
,, l. 53	gazer	filly gazer	innocent gazer
,, l. (67)	y'	you	[*not in*]
p. 37, l. 125	hungry	angrie	angry
,, l. 184	tis	twas	[*not in*]
,, l. (186)	ye	you	[,,]
p. 38, l. 196	his	your	his
,, l. 198	Yet	But	But
,, l. 198	eafe	cafe	eafe
,, l. 223	meantft :	meants,	meant'ft
p. 39, l. 225	thee downe	thy foule	thy Soule
,, l. 241	.	i	.
,, l. 241-3 *St. Dir. Salisburie*		Salbury	*Salisburie*
,, l. 244	That	The	[*not in*]
,, l. 280	kinde	louing	louing
p. 40, l. 327	fcritch-oules	fcrike-oules	Screech-Owles
p. 42, l. 17	poyfon	ftrong poifon	ftrong poyfon
,, l. 27	*Car.*	The Cardinall	[*not in*]
p. 43, l. 10	ranfome	ranfomes	ranfome
,, l. 37	Walter	Water	[*not in*]
p. 45, l. 15	elfe	more	[,,]

	Q3	Q1	F'1
p. 45, l. 31	be al	all be	[*not in*]
p. 46, l. 42	*Dicke*	Nicke	*But*
,, l. 44	Lacies	Brases	Lacies
,, l. 48	*Nicke*	VVill	*But.*
,, l. 54	the	for the	the
,, l. 56	becaufe	for	for
,, l. 56	no other	no	neuer a
,, l. 76	if	and if	and when
,, IV. ii. 7	come	comes	may come
p. 47, l. 99	Zounds	Sonnes [1]	Nay then
,, l. 106	ye	you	[*not in*]
,, l. 108	I . . ye	I can . . you	[,,]
,, l. 107	ore the	oth	on the
,, l. 109	What	And what	[*not in*]
,, l. 109	ye	you	thou
,, l. 112	truly	true	[*not in*]
,, l. 116	he has . . pen and inkehorne	hes . . . penny-inck-horne	He hath . . . Pen and Iuke-Horne
,, l. 131-3	*Cade* Then kneele downe Dicke Butcher. *He knights him* Rise vp sir Dicke Butcher. Now sound vp the drum[2]	He knights *Dicke Butcher.* *Cade.* Then kneele downe Dicke But-cher Rise vp sir Dicke Butcher. [As *St. Dir.*] Now sound vp the Drumme	[*not in*]
,, l. 140	a	but a	a
p. 48, l. 155	was	twas	'tis
,, l. 158	testifye it	testifie	testifie it
,, l. 173	crutch	crouch	ftaffe
p. 49, *St. Dir.*	I *where . . are both . . . enters*	and . . . is . . . enter	*wherein both . . . are* *Enter*
,, l. 8	, and thou	. Thou	and thou
p. 50, *St. Dir.*	*Sord . . . walking*	Lord . . walking. En-ter three or foure Citizens below.	*Lord . . . walking.* *Then enters two or three Citizens below.*
,, l. 11	will I	I will	I will
p. 51, l. 1	go	go fome	go fome
,, l. 2-3	Court	the Court	Court
,, IV. ii. 87	parchment fhould be made	fhould parchment be made	fhould be made Parchment
,, l. 137*	take	go with me, and take	[*not in*]
p. 52, l. 45	this	that	[,,]
,, l. 46	the Peace	Peace	Peace
,, l. 70	nor loft I	I loft not	I loft not
,, l. 99	at vs, as who wouldft	, as who,	as who fhould
p. 53, l. 137	quench	fquench	[*not in*]
,, l. 146	Your	You	[,,]
,, l. 148-9	he is . . on's	hees . . of his	[,,]
,, l. 150	and cut	cut	[,,]

[1] There are several instances of this form, tho' I give only one.
[2] The Stage Direction of Q1 is turnd into part of Cade's speech.

	Q3	Q1	F1
p. 53, l. 12	thefe	this	[*not in*]
p. 54, l. 22	ftraight way	ftraightwaies	[,,]
,, l. 36	fpeake	fpeak a word	[,,]
,, l. 65	wants	want ·	want
,, St. Dir. 2.	and flies	and then flies	[,,]
p. 55, l. 6	be	be it	[,,]
,, l. 13	thefe	that	[,,]
p. 56, l. 42	if	and I	if I
,, l. 45	fhall neuer	neuer fhall	fhall nere
,, l. 45	ftands	doth ftand	ftands
,, l. 52	with thee	thee	[*not in*]
,, l. 61	Would thou mightft	befeech God thou maift	befeech Ioue on my knees thou maift
,, l. 71	was this	was it	If't
,, l. 89	to the King	. . . .	to the King
p. 57, l. 39	then fo	but fo	[*alterd*]
p. 58, l. 65*	King *Henry*	Henry	[*not in*]
,, l. 78	Alexander	fir Alexander	[,,]
p. 59, l. 111	*King.*	Yorke.	*York*
p. 60, St. Dir.	*other doore,*	other	[*not in*]
p. 61, l. 66	tumble in thy blood	breathe thy laft	[,,]
,, St. Dir. 2	Alarmes	Alarme	[,,]
p. 62, l. 41*	I may	may I	[,,]
p. 63, l. 76*	fummon vp	fommon	[,,]
,, St. Dir. 3	*Yorke, Edward and*	*Yorke* and	*Yorke*
,, l. 12*	fpirited	fprited	[*not in*]
p. 64, l. 31	eterniz'd	eterneft	eterniz'd

§ 5. Now of all these changes, can any be set down to Shakspere? None, at first hand, I think. True that in I, p. iv, as in other cases, part of the changes made by the Q3 Revizer of Q1 are found in F1, but they are changes such as may have been made by a Revizer who heard the Folio Play (2 *Hen. VI.*) with a copy of Q1 or Q2 in his hand, or who had the chance of taking a note or two from the Burbage-playhouse copy, and then made further independent corrections at home. Shakspere was no doubt the revizer of Act I, scene ii, and Act II, scene ii, of 2 *Hen. VI.* from *The Con'ention* Q1, comprising all the main changes, I, II, III, IV, abuv.[1] He *may* of course have revized the ground-play twice; but if he did, his changes would surely have appeard in Q2, 1600, and not been kept back till 1619. The text of 2 *Hen. VI.* as it stands is so little like Shakspere's work after 1600, that I think we may safely conclude he had nothing to do directly with the Quarto of 1619.

§ 6. It will be useful to students to give here the statement which will be printed also in Q1, of Miss Jane Lee's assignment of the several parts of *The Contention*, 1594, to Marlowe and Greene,

---

[1] See Miss Jane Lee's Analysis of the play in *New. Sh. Soc. Trans.*, 1875-6, p. 293-4.

New Sh. Soc.'s Trans., 1875-6, p. 304-5. The two writers' work is broadly discernible by Marlowe's fuller and more sustaind line, and Greene's more choppy verse.

p. 3-6. 2 *Hen. VI*, I. i. (*Cont.* sc. i.), beginning "As by your high imperiall Maiesties command[1]," Marlowe and Greene together.

p. 6. 2 *Hen. VI*, I. ii. (*Cont.* sc. ii.), from "Why droopes my Lord like ouer ripened corne," Greene.

p. 9-14. 2 *Hen. VI*, I. iii. (*Cont.* sc. iii.): "Come sirs let vs linger here abouts a while," Greene, ll. 1-40; then Marlowe writes to l. 111; then Greene to end of scene.

p. 14-22. 2 *Hen. VI*, I. iv. to II. i. (*Cont.* sc. iv., v.): "Here Sir Iohn, take this scrole of paper here," Greene. "My Lord, how did your grace like this last flight," Greene.

p. 22-3. 2 *Hen. VI*, II. ii.-iv. (*Cont.* sc. vi.): "My Lords our simple supper ended, thus," Marlowe; but Warwick's part is perhaps written by Greene.

p. 23-5. 2 *Hen. VI*, II. vii., viii. (*Cont.* sc. vii., viii.): "Stand foorth Dame Elnor Cobham Duches of Gloster," Greene.

p. 27-31. 2 *Hen. VI*, III. i. (*Cont.* sc. ix.): "I wonder our vncle Gloster staies so long," Marlowe to l. 169, "Now York bethink thy self and rowse thee vp," when Greene takes it up and writes on to the end of the scene. Also, Greene may have written, or aided in writing, Humphrey's part in the previous lines.

p. 32-9. 2 *Hen. VI*, III. ii. (*Cont.* sc. x.): "How now sirs, what haue you dispatcht him?" Marlowe; though some of the wrens, ravens, basilisks, lambs, scorpions, partridges, puttocks, kites, lizards, serpents, screech-owls, were, I imagine, suggestions of Greene's.

p. 39. 2 *Hen. VI*, III. iii. (*Cont.* sc. xi.): "Oh death, if thou wilt let me liue but one whole yeare," Marlowe.

p. 43-7. 2 *Hen. VI*, IV. i., ii. (*Cont.* sc. xii., xiii.): "Bring forward these prisoners that scorn'd to yeeld," Greene.

p. 49. 2 *Hen. VI*, IV. iii. (*Cont.* sc. xiv.): Sir Dicke Butcher, thou hast fought to-day most valiantly," Greene.

p. 49-50. 2 *Hen. VI*, IV. iv. (*Cont.* sc. xv.): "Sir Humphrey Stafford and his brother is slaine," ? Greene—certainly not Marlowe.

p. 50-56. 2 *Hen. VI*, IV. v.-x. (*Cont.* sc. xvi.-xx.): "How now, is Iacke Cade flaine?" Greene.

p. 57-59. 2 *Hen. VI*, V. i. 1-115 (*Cont.* sc. xxi., xxii.): "In Armes from Ireland comes Yorke amaine," ? Greene—certainly not Marlowe.

p. 59-60. 2 *Hen. VI*, V. i. 124-216. "Long liue my noble Lord, and soueraigne King," Marlowe.

p. 61-4. 2 *Hen. VI*, V. ii., iii. (*Cont.* sc. xxiii.): "So Lie thou there, and breathe thy last" [Q1, and tumble in thy blood Q3], ll. 1-8, Greene; then Marlowe writes on to the end, except that Greene writes ll. 20-39.

§ 7. The transfer of the negatives to stone, and the printing of the text, have been done by a firm in Hamburg, in a way which contrasts delightfully with Messrs Unwin's disastrous failure with Quarto 1 of *Henry V.* But the original of *The Whole Contention* is in better condition than that of the Museum copy of *Henry V,* Q1.

---

[1] For the style and run of the lines in Henry's and Margaret's speeches to each other, cf. the passage beginning: "These gracious words most royal Carolus."—Faustus, IV. i.—JANE LEE.

THE
Whole Contention
betweene the two Famous
Houſes, L A N C A S T E R and
Y O R K E.

With the Tragicall ends of the good Duke
Humfrey, Richard Duke of Yorke,
and King Henrie the
ſixt.

Diuided into two Parts : And newly correcſed and
enlarged. Written by *William Shake-*
ſpeare, Gent.

Printed at L O N D O N, for T. P.

The firſt part of the Conten-
tion of the two *Famous Houſes of Yorke*
and Lancaſter, with the death of
the good Duke *Humfrey.*

Enter at one doore, King Henry the ſixt, and Humfrey Duke of Gloce-
ſter, the Duke of Somerſet, the Duke of Buckingham, Cardinall
Bewford, and others.

Enter at the other doore, the Duke of Yorke, and the Marques of Suf-
folke, and Queen Margaret, and the Earle of Saliſbury and War-
wicke.

Suffolke.

AS by your high Imperiall Maieſties command,
I had in charge at my depart for France,
As Procurator for your Excellence,
To marry Princes *Margaret* for your Grace;
So in the ancient famous Citty Towers,
In preſence of the Kings of *France* and *Cyſſile,*
The Dukes of *Orleance, Calabar, Britaine,* and *Alonſon.*
Seuen Earles, twelue Barons, and twenty reuerend Byſhops,
I did performe my taske, and was eſpouſd,
And now, moſt humbly on my bended knees,
In ſight of England and her royall Peeres,
Deliuer vp my title in the Queene
Vnto your gracious Excellence, that are the ſubſtance
Of that great ſhadow I did repreſent :
The happieſt gift that euer Marqueſſe gaue,
The faireſt Queene that euer King poſſeſt.

The

The contention of the two famous Houses

King. Suffolke arife.
Welcome Qveene *Margaret* to Englifh Henries Court,
The greateft fhew of kindneffe yet we can beftow,
Is this kinde kiffe: O gracious God of heauen,
Lend me a heart repleate with thankefulneffe,
For in this beauteous face thou haft beftowd
A world of pleafures to my perplexed foule.

Queene. Th'exceffiue loue I beare vnto your Grace,
Forbids me to be lauifh of my tongue,
Leaft I fhould fpeake more then befeemes a woman:
Let this fuffice, my bliffe is in your liking,
And nothing can make poore Margaret miferable,
Vnleffe the frowne of mighty Englands king.

King. Her lookes did wound, but now her fpeech doth pierce
Louely Queene Margaret fit downe by my fide:
And Vnkle Glofter, and you Lorldly Peeres,
With one voyce welcome my beloued Queene.

All. Long liue Queene Margaret, Englands happineffe.

Queene. VVe thanke you all.   *Sound trumpets*

Suffolke. My Lord Protector, fo it pleafe your Grace,
Heere are the Articles confirmd, of peace
Betweene our Soueraigne and the *French* king *Charles*,
Till terme of eighteene months be full expir'd.

Hum. Inprimis, It is agreed betweene the French king *Charles*
and *William de la Pole* Marqueffe of *Suffolke*, Embaffador for
Henry king of England, that the faide *Henry* fhal wed & efpoufe
the Lady *Margaret*, daughter to *Raynard* King of *Naples*, *Cyffels*,
and *Ierufalem*, and crowne her Queene of England, ere the thir-
ty day of the next month.

Item, It is further agreed betweene them, that the Dutcheffe
of *Anioy* and of *Maine*, fhall be releafed and deliuered ouer to
the King her fa———

Duke Humfrey lets it fall.

King. How now vnckle, whats the matter that you ftay fo fodainly.

Hum. Pardon my Lord, a fodaine qualme came ore my heart,
which dimmes mine eyes that I can reade no more.

My

of Yorke and Lancaster.

My Lord of Yorke, I pray do you reade on.

Yorke. Item, It is further agreed betweene them, that the Dutcheſſe of *Anioy* and of *Mayne*, ſhall bee releaſed and deliuered o-
uer to the King her father, and ſhe ſent ouer of the king of Englands owne proper coſt and charges, without dowry.

King. They pleaſe vs well, Lord Marqueſſe kneele downe: we
heere create thee firſt Duke of Suffolke, and girt thee with the
ſword. Coſin of Yorke, wee heere diſcharge your Grace from
being Regent in the parts of *France*, till terme of 18.months be
full expirde.

Thankes vnckle *Wincheſter*, *Gloſter*, *Yorke*, and *Buckingham*, So-
merſet, *Saliſbury*, and *Warwicke*.
We thanke you for all this great fauour done,
In entertainment to my Princely Queene,
Come let vs in, and with all ſpeede prouide
To ſee her Coronation be performd.

*Exit King, Queene, and Suffolke, & Duke Humphrey
ſtayes all the reſt.*

Hum. Braue Peeres of England, pillers of the State,
To you Duke *Humphrey* muſt vnfold his greefe,
What did my brother *Henry* toile himſelfe,
And waſte his ſubiects for to conquer *France*?
And did my brother *Bedford* ſpend his time,
To keepe in awe that ſtout vnruly Realme?
And haue not I and mine vnckle *Bewford* heere,
Done all we could to keepe that land in peace?
And is all our labours then ſpent quite in vaine?
For Suffolke he, the new made Duke that rules the roaſt,
Hath giuen away for our King *Henries* Queene,
The Dutcheſſe of *Anioy* and *Mayne* vnto her father.
Ah Lords, fatall is this marriage, cancelling our ſtates,
Reuerſing monuments of conquered *France*,
Vndoing all, as none had nere beene done.

Card. Why how now coſin Gloſter, what needs this?
As if our King were bound vnto your will,
And might not do his will without your leaue,
Proud Protector, enuy in thine eyes I ſee,

A 3   The

The big fwolne venome of thy hatefull heart,
That dares prefume gainſt that thy Soueraigne likes.

Hum. Nay my Lords, tis not my words that troubles you,
But my prefence, proud Prelate as thou art :
But ile be gone, and giue thee leaue to fpeake.
Farewell my Lords, and fay when I am gone,
I prophefied *France* would be loſt ere long.

Exit Duke Humfrey.

Card. There goes our Protector in a rage.
My Lords you know he is my great enemy,
And though he be Protector of the Land,
And thereby couers his deceitfull thoughts.
For you well fee, if he but walke the ſtreetes,
The common people fwarme about him ſtraight,
Crying Iefus bleſſe your royall excellence,
With God preferue the good Duke *Humfrey,*
And many things befides that are not knowne,
Which time will bring to light in fmooth duke *Humfrey.*
But I will after him, and if I can,
Ile lay a plot to heaue him from his feate.

Exit Cardinall.

Buck, But let vs watch this haughty Cardinall,
Cofin of Somerfet be rulde by me,
Weele watch duke *Humfrey* and the Cardinall too,
And put them from the marke they faine would hit.

Somer. Thankes cofin *Buckingham,* ioyne thou with me,
And both of vs with the duke of Suffolke,
Weele quickly heaue duke *Humfrey* from his feate.

Buck Content, come then let vs about it ſtraight,
For either thou or I will be Protector.

Exit Buckingham and Somerfet.

Sal. Pride went before, ambition followes after.
Whilſt thefe do feeke their owne preferments thus,
My Lords let vs feeke for our Conntries good:
Oft haue I feene this haughty Cardinall
Sweare, and forfweare himfelfe, and braue it out,
More like a Ruffian then a man of the Church.

Cofine

Yorke and Lancaster.

Cofin *Yorke*, the victories thou haft wonne,
In *Ireland*, *Normandy*, and in *France*,
Hath wonne thee immortall praife in England.
And thou braue *Warwicke*, my thrice valiant fonne,
Thy fimple plainneffe and thy houfe-keeping,
Hath won thee credit amongft the common fort,
The reuerence of mine age, and *Nevels* name,
Is of no little force if I command,
Then let vs ioyne all three in one for this,
That good duke *Humfrey* may his ftate poffeffe,
But wherefore weepes *Warwicke* my noble fonne.

War. For greefe that all is loft that *Warwicke* won,
Sonnes. Anioy and *Maine*, both giuen away at once,
Why *Warwick* did win them, & muft that then which we wonne
with our fwords, be giuen away with words.

Yorke. As I haue read, our Kings of England were wont to haue
large dowries with their wiues, but our king *Henry* giues a-
way his owne.

Salf. Come fonnes away and looke vnto the maine.

War. Vnto the *Maine*, Oh father *Maine* is loft,
Which *Warwicke* by maine force did vvin from France,
Maine chance father you meant, but I meant *Maine*,
Which I vvill vvin from France, or elfe bee flaine.

                        Exit Salisbury and Warwicke.

Yorke. Anioy and *Maine*, both giuen vnto the French,
Cold nevves for me, for I had hope of *France*,
Euen as I haue of fertile England.
A day will come when *Yorke* fhall claime his owne,
And therefore I will take the *Nevels* parts,
And make a fhew of loue to proud duke *Humfrey* :
And when I fpy aduantage, claime the Crowne,
For thats the golden marke I feeke to hit :
Nor fhall proud *Lancaster* vfurpe my right,
Nor hold the Scepter in his childifh fift,
Nor weare the diadem vpon his head,
Whofe Church-like humors fits not for a Crowne :
Then *Yorke* be ftill a while till time doe ferue,

                              Watch

† 191
†
†
† 187
↓
†
†
＊
†
†
† 112
†
† 116
†
† 119
† 125
†
† 205
†
209
233
236
240
244

Watch thou, and wake when others be afleepe,
To pry into the fecrets of the ftate,
Till *Henry* furfetting in ioyes of loue,
With his new Bride, and Englands deere bought Queene,
And *Humfrey* with the Peeres be falne at iarres,
Then will I raife aloft the milke-white Rofe,
With whofe fweet fmell the ayre fhall be perfumde,
And in my Standard beare the Armes of *Yorke*,
To grapple with the houfe of *Lancaſter* :
And force perforce, ile make him yeelde the Crowne,
Whofe bookiſh rule hath Puld faire England downe.

Exit Yorke.

Enter Duke Humfrey, and Dame Ellanor,
Cobham his wife.

Elnor. Why droopes my Lord like ouer-ripened Corne,
Hanging the head at Ceres plenteous load,
What feeſt thou Duke *Humfrey* King *Henries* Crowne?
Reach at it, and if thine arme bee too fhort,
Mine fhall lengthen it. Art thou not a Prince?
Vnckle to the King? and his Protector?
Then what fhouldſt thou lacke that might content thy minde?
  Hum. My louely *Nell,* farre be it from my heart,
To thinke of treafons gainſt my Soueraigne Lord,
But I was troubled with a dreame to night,
And God I pray, it do betide none ill.
  Elnor. What dreamt my Lord? Good *Humfrey* tell it me,
And ile interpret it : and when thats done,
Ile tell thee then what I did dreame to night.
  Hum. This night when I was laid in bed, I dreamt
That this my ſtaffe, mine Office badge in Court,
Was broke in twaine, by whom I cannot geſſe:
But as I thinke by the Cardinall. What it bodes
God knowes ; and on the ends were plac'd
The heads of *Edmund* Duke of *Somerſet,*
And *William de la Pole* firſt Duke of *Suffolke.*

Elnor. Tuſt

Elnor. Tuſh my Lord, this ſignifies nought but this.
That he that breakes a ſticke of Gloſters groue,
Shall for the offence make forfet of his head.
But now my Lord ile tell you what I dreamt,
Methought I was in the Cathedrall Church
At Weſtminſter, and ſeated in the chaire
Where Kings and Queenes are crown'd, and at my feete
Henry and *Margaret* with a Crowne of Gold,
Stood ready to ſet it on my Princely head.

Hum. Fie *Nell.* Ambitious woman as thou art,
Art thou not ſecond woman in this land,
And the Protectors wife ? belou'd of him ?
And wilt thou ſtill be hammering treaſon thus?
A way I ſay, and let me heare no more.

Elnor. How now my Lord, what angry with your *Nell*
For telling but her dreame ? The next I haue
Ile keepe it to my ſelfe, and not be rated thus,

Hum. Nay *Nell*, ile giue no credit to a dreame,
But I would haue thee to thinke on no ſuch things.

Enter a Meſſenger.

Meſſ. And it pleaſe your Grace, the King and Queen to morrow morning will ride a hawking to S. Albones, & craues your
company along with them.

Hum. With all my heart ; I will attend his Grace.
Come *Nell*, thou wilt go with vs I am ſure.

Exit Humfrey.

Elnor. Ile come after you, for I cannot go before,
As long as Gloſter beares this baſe and humble minde :
Were I a man, and Protector as he is,
I'de reach to'th Crowne, or make ſome hop headleſſe.
And being but a woman, ile not behinde
For playing of my part, in ſpite of all that ſeek to croſſe me thus:
Who is within there?

Enter Sir Iohn Hum.

What Sir *Iohn Hum*, what newes with you ?

B   *Sir Iohn.*

10.

2 Hen. VI.

I. ii.

+ 70

†

† 72

†

†

- 76

†

†

† 80

†

✶

✶

✶

✶

✶

✶

✶

✶

✶

✶

The contention of the two famous Houſes,

Sir Iohn. Ieſus preſerue your Maieſty.

Elnor. My Maieſty : why man, I am but Grace.

Sir Iohn. I, but by the grace of God, and *Hums* aduice,
Your Graces ſtate ſhall be aduanc'd ere long.

Elnor. What, haſt thou conferr'd with *Margery Iourdain,* the
cunning witch of *Rye,* with *Roger Bullenbrooke* and the reſt ? and
will they vndertake to do me good ?

Sir Iohn. I haue Madam, and they haue promiſed me to raiſe
a ſpirit from depth of vnder ground, that ſhall tell your Grace
all queſtions you demand.

Elnor. Thankes good ſir *Iohn.*
Some two dayes hence I geſſe will fit our time,
Then ſee that they be heere :
For now the King is riding to Saint *Albones,*
And all the Dukes and Earles along with him.
When they be gone, then ſafely may they come,
And on the backe ſide of my Orchard heere,
There caſt their **Spelles** in ſilence of the night,
And ſo reſolue vs of the thing we wiſh ;
Till when, drinke that for my ſake, and ſo farewell.

Exit Elanor.

Sir Iohn. Now ſir *Iohn Hum,* No words but mum.
Seale vp your lips, for you muſt ſilent be :
Theſe gifts ere long will make me mighty rich.
The Dutcheſſe ſhe thinkes now that all is well,
But I haue Gold comes from another place,
From one that hyred me to ſet her on,
To plot theſe treaſons gainſt the King and Peeres ;
And that is the mighty Duke of Suffolke.
For he it is, but I muſt not ſay ſo,
That by my meanes muſt worke the Dutcheſſe fall,
Who now by Coniurations thinkes to riſe.
But whiſt ſir *Iohn,* no more of that I tro,
For feare you loſe your head before you go. *Exit*

Enter two Petitioners, and Peter the Armourers man.

1. *Petit.* Come ſirs lets linger here abouts a while,

Vntill

Yorke and Lancaster.

Vntill my Lord Protector come this way,

That we may shew his Grace our seuerall causes.

　2.*Petit.* I pray God saue the Good Duke *Humfries* life,

For but for him a many were vndone,

That cannot get no succour in the Court.

But see where he comes with the Queene.

> *Enter the Duke of Suffolke with the Queene, and they take*
> *him for Duke Humfrey, and giues*
> *him their writings.*

　1.*Petit.* Oh we are vndone, this is the Duke of Suffolke.

　Queene. Now good-fellows, whom would you speak withal?

　2. *Petit.* If it please your Maiestie, with my Lord Protectors

Grace.

　Qu. Are your suites to his Grace? Let vs see them first,

Looke on them my Lord of Suffolke.

　Suffolke. A Complaint against the Cardinals man.

What hath he done?

　2. *Petit.* Marry my Lord, he hath stole away my wife,

And th'are gone together, and I know not where to finde them.

　Suff. Hath he stole thy wife? that's some iniury indeede.

But what say you?

　Peter Thumpe. Marry sir I come to tell you, that my Mayster

saide, that the Duke of Yorke was true heire to the Crown, and

that the King was an vsurer.

　Queene. An vsurper thou wouldst say.

　Peter. I forsooth, an vsurper.

　Queene. Didst thou say the King was an vsurper?

　Peter. No forsooth, I saide my maister saide so, th'other day

when wee were scowring the Duke of Yorkes armour in our

Garret.

　Suf. I marry, this is something like,

Who's within there?

> *Enter one or two.*

Sirra, take in this fellow, and keepe him close,

　　　　B 2　　　　　　　　　　　　　　　　And

† 2

† 3

†

†

"

† 7-8

† 9-10

† 11-12

† 14

†

† 16-17

†

† 19

†

† 20

†

† 22

†

† 28-9

† 30

† 34-5

†

†

†

† 33

† 193

194

†

† 36

† 37

†37 And send out a Purseuant for his master straight,

†38-9 Weele heere more of this thing before the King.

Exit with the Armorers man.

†23 Now Sir, what's yours? Let me see it,

What's heere?

†24 A complaint against the Duke of Suffolke, for enclosing the

† commons of long Melford.

25 How now sir knaue.

† ·1.*Petit.* I beseech your Grace to pardon me, I am but a Mes-

†27 senger for the whole towne-ship.

He teares the Papers.

†42 *Suffolke.* So now shew your petitions to Duke *Humfrey.*

٭ Villaines get you gone, and come not neere the Court,

٭ Dare these pesants write against me thus?

Exit Petitioners.

†45 *Queene.* My Lord of Suffolke you may see by this,

٭ The Commons loues vnto that haughty Duke,

†49 That seekes to him more then to King *Henry*:

٭ Whose eyes are alwaies poring on his booke,

٭ And nere regards the honor of his name,

†II. iii. 29 But still must be protected like a childe,

٭ And gouerned by that ambitious Duke,

٭· That scarse will mooue his cap to speake to vs,

†79 And his proud wife, high-minded *Elanor,*

†80 That ruffles it with such a troope of Ladies,

†82 As strangers in the Court take her for *Queene*:

†83 She beares a Dukes whole reuennewes on her backe.

†87 The other day she vanted to her maides,

١ That the very traine of her worst gowne,

†89 Was worth more wealth then all my fathers landes.

٭ Can any greefe of minde be like to this?

†53 I tell thee *Pole,* when thou didst run at Tilt,

†55 And stolst away our Ladies hearts in France,

†56 I thought King *Henry* had bene like to thee,

٭ Or else thou hadst not brought me out of France.

†68 *Suff.* Madam, content your selfe a little while,

†69 As I was cause of your comming into England,

Yorke and Lancaster.

So will I in England worke your full content:
And as for proud Duke *Humfrey* and his wife,
I haue fet lime· twigs that will entangle them,
As that your Grace ere long fhall vnderftand,
But ftay Madame, heere comes the King.

Enter King Henrie, and the Duke of Yorke and the Duke of Sommer-
fet on both fides of the King, whifpering with him: Then entereth
Duke Humphrey, Dame Elanor, the Duke of Buckingham, the
Earle of Salisbury, the Earle of Warwicke, and the Cardinall of
Winchefter.

King. My Lords I care not who be Regent in *France*, or *Yorke*
or *Somerfet*, all's one to me.

Yorke. My Lord, if *Torke* haue ill demean'd himfelfe,
Let *Somerfet* enioy his place, and go to Fraunce.

Som. Then whom your grace thinkes worthy, let him goe,
And there be made the Regent ouer the French.

Warwicke. Whomfoeuer you account worthy,
Torke is the worthieft.

Card. Peace *Warwicke*, giue thy betters leaue to fpeake.

War. The Cardnal's not my better in the fielde.

Buck. All in this place are thy betters farre.

War. And *Warwicke* may liue to be beft of all.

Queene. My Lord in mine opinion, it were beft that *Somerfet*
were Regent ouer France.

Hum. Madame, our King is olde enough himfelfe,
To giue his anfwer without your confent.

Queene. If he be old enough, what needs your Grace
To be Protector ouer him fo long.

Hum. Madam, I am but Protector ore the Land,
And when it pleafe his Grace, I will refigne my charge.

Suffolke. Refigne it then, for fince thou waft a King
(As who is King but thee:) the common ftate
Doth as we fee, all wholly go to wracke,
And Millions of treafure hath beene fpent,
And as for the Regentfhip of France,

B3   I

The Contention of the two famous Houses,

I fay *Somerfet* is more worthy then *Yorke.*

Yorke, Ile tell thee *Suffolke* why I am not worthy,
Becaufe I cannot flatter as thou canft.

War. And yet the worthy deeds that *Yorke* hath done,
Should make him worthy to be honoured heere.

Suf. Peace head-ftrong *Warwicke.*

War. Image of pride, wherefore fhould I peace?

Suf. Becaufe heere is a man accufde of Treafon,
Pray God the Duke of *Yorke* do cleare himfelfe.
Ho, bring hither the Armourer and his man.

Enter the Armourer and his man.

If it pleafe your Grace, this fellow here, hath accufed his mafter
of high Treafon, and his wordes were thefe : That the Duke of
Yorke was lawfull heire vnto the Crowne, and that your Grace
was an vfurper.

Yorke. I befeech your Grace let him haue what punnifhment
the Law will affoord for his villany.

King. Come hither fellow, didft thou fpeake thefe words ?

Arm. An't fhall pleafe your worfhip, I neuer fayde any fuch
matter, God is my witneffe, I am falfely accufed by this villen
heere.

Peter. Tis no matter for that, you did fay fo.

Yorke. I befeech your Grace, let him haue the Law.

Armorer, Alas mafter, hang me if euer I fpake the words. My
accufer is my prentice, and when I did correct him for his fault
the other day, he did vow vpon his knees that he wuuld be euen
with mee : I haue good witneffe of this, and therefore I befeech
your worfhip do not caft away an honeft man for a villaines ac-
cufation.

King. Vncle Glofter, what do you thinke of this ?

Hum. The law my Lord is this by cafe, it refts fufpitious,
That a day of combate be appointed,
And there to try each others right or wrong,
With *Eben* ftaues and Sandbags, combatting
In *Smithfield,* before your royall Maiefty   *Exit Humfrey.*

Armour. And I accept the combate willingly.

                                                          Peter

Yorke and Lancaster.

Peter. Alaſſe my Lord, I am not able for to fight.

Suf. You muſt either fight ſirra, or elſe be hang'd :
Go take them hence againe to priſon. *Exit with them.*

The Queene lets fall her gloue, and hits the Dutcheſſe of
Gloſter, a boxe on the eare.

Queene. Giue me my gloue. Why Minion can you not ſee ?
Shee ſtrikes her.
I cry you mercy Madam, I did miſtake,
I did not thinke it had bene you.

Elnor. Did you not proud French-woman ?
Could I come neere your dainty viſage with my nayles,
I'de ſet my ten command'ments in your face.

King. Be patient gentle Aunt,
It was againſt her will.

Elnor. Againſt her will. Good King ſhee'll dandſe thee,
If thou wilt alwayes thus be rul'd by her,
But let it reſt : as ſure as I do liue,
She ſhall not ſtrike Dame *Elnor* vnreueng'd.

Exit Elnor.

King. Beleeue me my loue, thou wert much too blame :
I would not for a thouſand pounds of Gold,
My Noble Vnckle had beene heere in place.

Enter Duke Humfrey.

But ſee where he comes : I am glad he met her not.
Vnkle Gloſter, what anſwer makes your Grace,
Concerning our Regent for the Realme of France,
Whom thinkes your Grace is meeteſt for to ſend.

Hum. My gracious Lord, then this is my reſolue,
For that theſe words the Armourer ſhould ſpeake,
Doth breede ſuſpition on the part of Yorke,
Let Somerſet be Regent ore the French,
Till trials made, and Yorke may cleare himſelfe.

King. Then be it ſo, my Lord of Somerſet,
We make your Grace Regent ouer the French,
And to defend our right 'gainſt forraine foes,

And

And so do good vnto the Realme of France,
Make hast my Lord, tis time that you were gone,
The time of truce I thinke is full expir'd.

   Somer. I humbly thanke your royall Maiesty,
And take my leaue to poste with speed to France.

                                Exit Somerset.

   King. Come Vnkle Gloster, now let's haue our horse,
For we will to Saint *Albones* presently.
Madam your Hawke they say is swift of flight,
And we will try how she will flye to day.   *Exit omnes.*

    Enter Elanor, with Sir Iohn Hum, Roger Bullenbrooke a Coniurer,
            and Margery Iourdaine a Witch.

   Elnor. Heere sir *Iohn,* take this scrole of paper here,
Wherein is writ the questions you shall aske,
And I will stand vpon this Tower heere,
And heare the spirit what it sayes to you :
And to my questions, write the answers downe.

            She goes vp to the Tower.
   Sir Iohn. Now sirs begin, and cast your spels about,
And charme the fiendes for to obey your wils,
And tell Dame *Elnor* of the thing she askes.

   Witch. Then *Roger Bullenbrooke* about thy taske,
And frame a circle heere vpon the earth,
Whilst I thereon all prostrate on my face,
Do talke and whisper with the Diuels below,
And coniure them for to obey my will.

               Shee lyes downe vpon her face.
        Bullenbrooke makes a Circle.
   Bullen. Darke night, dread night, the silence of the night,
Wherein the Furies maske in hellish troupes,
Send vp I charge you from *Sosetus* Lake,
The spirit *Ascalon* to come to mee,
To pierce the bowels of this Centricke earth,
And hither come in twinkling of an eye,

                            Ascalon

Yorke and Lancaster.

Afcalon, Affenda, affenda.
*It Thunders and Lightens, and then the spirite
rifeth vp.*

Spirit. Now *Bullenbrooke* what wouldst thou haue me doe? † 31
Bullen. First of the King, what shall become of him? †
Spirit. The Duke yet liues, that *Henry* shall depose,
But him out-liue, and dye a violent death. 34
Bullen. What fate awaites the Duke of *Suffolke.* †
Spirit. By water shall he die, and take his end. 36
Bullen. What shall betide the Duke of *Somerfet* ? †
Spirit. Let him shun Castles, safer shall he be vpon the sandy
plaines, then where Castles mounted stand : † 40
Now question me no more, for I must hence againe. †

He sinkes downe againe.

Bullen. Then downe I say, vnto the damned poole, ✳
Where Pluto in his fiery waggon sits, ✳
Riding amidst the sindg'd and parched smoakes, ✳
The rode of *Dytas* by the Riuer Stix : ✳
There howle and burne for euer in those flames, ✳
Rise *Ionrdaine* rise, and stay thy charming Spels. ✳
Zounds, we are betraide. ✳

*Enter the Duke of Yorke, and the Duke of Bucking-
ham, and others.*

Yorke. Come sirs, lay hands on them, and binde them sure. † 44
This time was well watcht. What Madame are you there . † 45-6
This will be great credit for your husband, ✳
That you are plotting treasons thus with Coniurers, ✳
The King shall haue notice of this thing. † 46
      Exit Elnor about.
Buck. See heere my Lord, what the diuell hath writ. † 60
Yorke. Giue it me my Lord, Ile shew it to the King. ✳
Go sirs, see them fast lockt in prison. † 53
      Exit with them.
Bucking. My Lord, I pray you let me go poste vnto the King, † 76
Vnto S. Albones, to tell this newes.
Yorke. Content. Away then, about it straight. ✳
            C   *Bucke*

I. ix.

*

82

*

83

84

*

Buck. Farewell my Lord.

Exit Buckingham.

Yorke. Whofe within there?

Enter one.

One. My Lord.

Yorke. Sirrah, go will the Earles of Salsbury and Warwick to fup with me to night.

Exit Torke.

One. I will my Lord.

Exit.

II. i. †

†

*

†3

†4

†7

†

†6

*

†9

†11-12

†

†

†

†16

17

†

20-1

*

†25-6

†21-8

†

†

†31

Enter the King and Queene with her Hawke on her fift, and Duke Humfrey and Suffolke, and the Cardinall, as if they came from Hawking.

Queene. My Lord, how did your grace like this laft flight?
But as I caft her off the winde did rife,
And twas ten to one, old Ione had not gone out.

King. How wonderfull the Lords workes are on earth,
Euen in thefe filly creatures of his hands,
Vnkle Glofter, how hye your hawke did fore,
And on a fodaine fouc'd the Partridge downe.

Suff. No maruell if it pleafe your Maiefty,
My Lord Protectors hawkes do towre fo well.
They know their mafter fores a Faulcons pitch.

Hum. Faith my Lord, it's but a bafe minde,
That fores no higher then a bird can fore.

Card. I thought your Grace would be aboue the clouds.

Hum. I my Lord Cardinall, were it not good
Your grace could fly to heauen.

Card. Thy heauen is on earth, thy words and thoughts beate
on a Crowne, proud Protector, dangerous Peere, to fmoothe it
thus with King and Gommonwealth.

Hum. How now my Lord, why this is more then needs, church
men fo hot? Good vnckle can you do't.

Suf. Why not, hauing fo good a quarrell, and fo bad a caufe?

Hum. As how, my Lord?

Suf. As you, my Lord, and t'like your Lordly Lordes Protectorfhip.

Hum. Why Suffolke, England knowes thy infolence.

Queene.

Yorke and Lancaster.

Queene. And thy ambition Gloſter,

King. Ceaſe gentle Queene, and whette not on theſe furious Lords to wrath, for bleſſed are the peace-makers on earth.

Card. Let me be bleſſed for the peace I make, Againſt this proud Protector with my ſword.

Hum. Faith holy Vnkle, I would it were come to that.

Card. Euen when thou dar'ſt.

Hum. Dare: I tel thee Prieſt, Plantagenets could neuer brook the dare.

Card. I am Plantagenet as well as thou, and ſonne to Iohn of Gaunt.

Hum. In baſtardy.

Card: I ſcorne thy words.

Hum: Make vppe no factious numbers, but euen in thine owne perſon meete me at the Eaſt end of the groue.

Card: Here's my hand, I will.

King: Why how now Lords?

Card, Faith Coſin Gloſter, had not your man caſt off ſo ſoone, we had had more ſport to day, Come with thy ſword and Buck-ler.

Hum: Gods mother Prieſt Ile ſhaue your crowne.

Card: Protector, protect thy ſelfe well.

King The winde growes high, ſo dothy our choller Lords.

Enter one crying a miracle, a miracle.

How now? Now ſirra, what miracle is it?

One. And it pleaſe your Grace, there is a man that came blind to S. Albones, and hath receiued his ſight at the ſhrine.

King Go fetch him hether, that wee may glorifie the lord with him.

Enter the Maior of Saint Albones, and his Brethren, with Mu-ficke, bearing the man that had bene blind between two in a chaire

King: Thou happy man, giue God eternall praiſe, For he it is that thus hath helped thee: Where waſt thou borne?

Poore man. At *Barwicke* pleaſe your Maieſty in the North.

C2   *Hum.*

*

† 90

† 91

† 95

†

† 96

†

† 98

† 99

† 102

† 97-8

*

*

*·

† 80

81

† 106

† 107

† 108

† 110

*

*·

*

*

† 111

†

†·

114

† 115

† 117

120

121

*

*

The contention of the two famous Houses,

Hum. At Barwicke, and come thus farre for helpe.

Poore man. I fir, it was told me in my fleepe,

That fweete Saint Albones fhould giue me my fight againe.

Hum. What are lame too?

P.man, I indeede fir, God helpe me.

Hum. How camft thou lame?

P. man. With falling off a plum tree.

Hum. Wert thou blind & would climb plumtrees?

P. man. Neuer but once fir in all my life,

My wife did long for plummes.

Hum. But tell me, wert thou borne blinde?

P.man. I truly fir.

Woman. I indeed fir, he was borne blinde.

Hum. What art thou his mother?

Woman. His wife fir.

Hum. Hadft thou beene his mother,

Thou couldft haue better tolde.

Why let me fee, I thinke thou canft not fee yet.

P.man. Yes truly mafter, as cleare as day.

Hum. Sayft thou fo: what colour's his cloake?

P. man, Red mafter, as red as blood.

Hum. And his cloake?

P. man. Why that's greene.

Hum. And what colour's his hofe?

P. man. Yellow mafter, yellow as gold.

Hum. And what colour's my Gowne?

P.man. Blacke fir, as blacke as Iet.

King. Then belike he knowes what colour iet is on.

Suf. And yet I thinke Iet did he neuer fee.

Hum. But clokes & gowns ere this day many a one.

But tell me firra, what's my name?

P.man. Alas mafter I know not.

Hum. What's his name?

P.man. I know not.

Hum. Nor his?

P.man. No truly fir.

Hum. Nor his name?

                                                    P. man

of Yorke and Lancaster.

P.man. No indeede maſter.

Hum. Whats thine owne name?

P.man. Sander, and it pleaſe you maiſter.

Hum. Then Sander ſit there, the lyingeſt knaue in Chriſten-
dom. If thou hadſt bene borne blinde, thou mightſt aſwel haue
knowne all our names, as thus to name the ſeuerall colours wee
do weare. Sight may diſtinguiſh of colours, but ſodainly to no-
minate them all, it is impoſſible. ✦ My Lords, ↑ S. Albones heere
hath done a miracle, & would you not think his cunning to bee
great, that could reſtore this Cripple to his legs againe.

P.man. Oh maſter I would you could.

Hum. My Maſters of S. Albones,
Haue you not Beadles in your Towne,
And things call'd whippes?

Mayor. Yes my Lord, if it pleaſe your Grace.

Hum. Then ſend for one preſently.

Maior. Sirra, go fetch the Beadle hither ſtraight. *Exit one.*

Hum. Now fetch me a ſtoole hither by and by.
Now ſirra, if you meane to ſaue your ſelfe from whipping,
Leape me ouer this ſtoole, and runne away.

Enter a Beadle.

P.man. Alas maſter I am not able to ſtand alone,
You go about to torture me in vaine.

Hum. VVell ſir, we muſt haue you finde your legges,
Sirra Beadle, whip him till he leape ouer that ſame ſtoole.

Beadle. I will my Lord, come on ſirra, off with your Doublet
quickly.

Poore man. Alas maſter what ſhall I do, I am not able to ſtand.

*After the Beadle hath hit him one ierke, he leapes ouer the ſtoole, and
runnes away, and they run after him, crying a Myracle, a Myracle.*

Hum. A miracle, a miracle, let him be taken againe, and whipte
through euery Market Towne till he comes at Barwicke where
he was borne.

Maior. It ſhall be done my Lord. *Exit Mayor.*

Suf. My Lord Protector hath done wonders to day,

C 3 　　　　　　　　　　　　Hee

122

†124

128

132

†

135

137

140-1

144

149

143-9

153

†138

161

II.i.
†162
†163-4

*
*

†165
*
†169
†171
†172
†174
*
*
*
†I.iv.60 *
*I.iv.32
*I.iv.33
* 34
*
*I.iv.35
*I.iv.36
*
*
*I.iv.37 8
*I.iv.39
*I.iv.40
†178
†180
†
†182-3
*
*
†192
*
†197

The contention of the two famous Houses,

He hath made the blinde to see, and halt to goe.

  Humph. I, but you did greater wonders, whē you made whole
Dukedomes flye in a day.

Witnesse France.

  King. Haue done I say, and let me heare no more of that.

      Enter the Duke of Buckingham.

What newes brings Duke *Humfrey* of *Buckingham?*

  Buck. Ill newes for some my Lord, and this it is,
That proud dame *Elnor* our Protectors Wife,
Hath plotted Treasons gainst the King and Peeres,
By witchcrafts, sorceries, and coniurings,
Who by such meanes did raise a spirit vp,
To tell her what hap should betide the State,
But ere they had finisht their diuellish drift,
By *Yorke* and my selfe they were all surprizde,
And heeres the answere the diuell did make to them.

  King. First of the King, what shall become of him?

  Reads. The Duke yet liues, that *Henry* shall depose,
Yet him out-liue, and die a violent death.
Gods will be done in all.
What fate awaits the Duke of Suffolke?
By water shall he die and take his end.

  Suffolke. By water must the Duke of *Suffolke* die?
It must be so, or else the diuell doth lie.

  King. Let *Somerset* shun Castles,
For safer shall he be vpon the sandy plaines,
Then where Castles mounted stand.

  Card. Heeres good stuffe, how now my Lord Protector,
This newes I thinke hath turnd your weapons point,
I am in doubt youle scarsely keepe your promise.

  Humph. Forbeare ambitious Prelate to vrge my greefe,
And pardon me my gracious Soueraigne,
For heere I sweare vnto your Maiesty,
That I am guiltlesse of these hainous crimes
Which my ambitious wife hath falsly done,
And for she would betray her soueraigne Lord,
I heere renounce her from my bed and boord,

                                  And

of Yorke and Lancaster.

And leaue her open for the law to iudge, † 198

Vnlesse she cleare her selfe of this foule deed.

    *King.*Come my Lords, this night weele lodge in S.*Albones,* † 200

And to morrow we will ride to London, † 201

And trie the vtmost of these treasons forth, † 203

Come vnckle Gloster along with vs,

My minde doth tell me thou art innocent. +III.i.141

                Exit omnes.

    Enter the Duke of Yorke, and the Earles of Salisbury
            and Warwicke.

    *Yorke.*My Lords, our simple supper ended thus, † 1-2

Let me reueale vnto your honors heere, † 2-4

The right and title of the house of Yorke † 4

To Englands Crowne by lineall desent. † 5

    *War.*Then Yorke begin,and if thy claime be good, † 7 8

The Neuils are thy subiects to command. †

    *Yorke.*Then thus my Lords, †

Edward the third had seuen sonnes,

The first was *Edward* the blacke Prince, †

Prince of *Wales.*

The second was *William* of *Hatfield,* †12

Who dyed young.

The third was *Lyonell,*Duke of *Clarence.* †13

The fourth was *Iohn of Gaunt,* †

The Duke of *Lancaster.*

The fift was *Edmund of Langley,* †14

Duke of Yorke.

The sixt was *William* of *Windsore,* †16

Who dyed young.

§ The seauenth and last was Sir *Thomas of Woodstocke,* Duke of †17.16

§   *Yorke.*

Now *Edward* the blacke Prince dyed before his Father, leauing †18

behinde him two sonnes, *Edward* borne at *Angolesme,* who died †

young,and *Richard* that was after crowned King,by the name of †19.20

Richard the second,who dyed without an heyre. †33

                      Lyonell

Lyonell Duke of Clarence dyed, and left him one only daughter, named *Phillip*, who was married to Edmund Mortimer earle of March and Vlster: and so by her I claime the Crowne, as the true heire to Lyonell Duke of Clarence, third sonne to Edward the third. Now sir, in time of Richards reigne, Henry of Bullingbrooke, sonne and heire to Iohn of Gaunt, the Duke of Lancaster fourth sonne to Edward the third, he claim'd the Crowne, depos'd the Meethfull King, and as both you know, in Pomfret Castle harmelesse Richard was shamefully murthered, and so by Richards death came the house of Lancaster vnto the Crowne.

Sal. Sauing your tale my Lord, as I haue heard in the reigne of Bullenbrooke, the Duke of Yorke did claime the Crowne, and but for Owen Glendour had bene King.

Yorke. True: but so it fortuned then, by meanes of that monstrous rebell Glendour, the noble Duke of Yorke was putte to death, and so euer since the heires of Iohn of Gaunt haue possessed the Crowne. But if the issue of the elder should succeed before the issue of the younger, then am I lawfull heire vnto the Kingdome.

Warwicke. VVhat proceedings can be more plain, he claimes it from Lyonell Duke of Clarence, the third sonne to Edward the third, and Henry from Iohn of Gaunt the fourth sonne. So that till Lionels issue failes, his should not reigne. It fayles not yet, but flourisheth in thee and in thy sonnes, braue slips of such a stocke. Then noble father, kneele we both together, & in this priuate place, be we the first to honour him with birth-right to the Crowne.

Both. Long liue Richard Englands royall King.

Yorke. I thanke you both. But Lords I am not your King, vntil this sword be sheathed euen in the hart blood of the house of Lancaster.

War. Then Yorke aduise thy selfe, and take thy time,
Claime thou the Crowne, and set thy standard vp,
And in the same aduance the milke-white Rose,
And then to guard it, will I rowse the Beare,
Enuiron'd with ten thousand Ragged staues,
To aide and helpe thee for to win thy right,

Mauger

Yorke and Lancaſter.

Mauger the proudeſt Lord of *Henries* blood,
That dares deny the right and claime of *Yorke*,
For why,my minde preſageth I ſhall liue
To ſee the noble Duke of *Yorke* to be a King.

   *Yorke.*Thanks noble *Warwicke*,and *Yorke* doth hope to ſee,
The Earle of *Warwicke* liue, to bee the greateſt man in England,
but the King. Come lets goe.

                             Exit omnes.

Enter King Henry and the Queene,Duke Humfrey,the Duke of Suf-
folke,and the Duke of Buckingham, the Cardinall, and Dame El-
nor Cobham,led with the Officers,and then enter to them the Duke
of Yorke,and the Earles of Salisbury and Warwicke.

   *King.*Stand forth Dame *Elnor Cobham* Dutches of *Gloſter*,and
heare the ſentence pronounced againſt thee for theſe treaſons,
that thou haſt committed gainſt Vs,our State and Peeres.

   Firſt for thy hainous crime, thou ſhalt two dayes in London
do pennance barefoot in the ſtreetes, with a white ſheete about
thy body, and a waxe Taper burning in thy hand. That done,
thou ſhalt be baniſhed for euer into the Iſle of Man,there to end
thy wretched daies ; and this is our ſentence irreuocable. Away
with her.

   *Elnor.*Euen to my death,for I haue liued too long.

                     Exit ſome with Elnor.

   *King.*Greeue not noble Vnckle,but be thou glad,
In that theſe treaſons thus are come to light,
Leaſt God had pourde his vengeance on thy head,
For her offences that thou heldſt ſo deare.

   *Humph.*Oh gracious *Henry*,giue me leaue a while,
To leaue your Grace,and to depart away,
For ſorrowes teares hath gripte my aged heart,
And makes the fountaines of mine eyes to ſwell,
And therefore good my Lord,let me depart.

   *King.*With all my hart good vnckle,whē you pleaſe
Yet ere thou goeſt, *Humfrey* reſigne thy ſtaffe,
For *Henry* will be no more protected,
The Lord ſhall be my guide both for my land and me.

               D   *Humph.*

✶
✶
† 77-8
† 79
✶
† 81-2
| 82

† 1
† 3
✶
| 11
† 11
✶
† 13
✶
✶
† 14

✶
✶
✶
✶
† 20
✶
† 18
† 17
† 20
✶
† 22-3
† 23
| 24

The contention of the two famous Houses,

Hum. My ftaffe, I noble Henry, my life and all,
My ftaffe, I yeelde as willing to be thine,
As ere thy Noble father made it mine :
And euen as willing at thy feete I leaue it,
As others would ambitioufly receiue it,
And long hereafter, when I am dead and gone,
May honourable peace attend thy throne.
King. Vnkle Glofter, ftand vp and go in peace,
No lefle belou'd of vs, then when
Thou wert Proteƈtor ouer this my land.   *Exit Glofter.*
Queene. Take vp the ftaffe, for heere it ought to ftand,
Where fhould it be, but in King Henries hand?
Yorke. Pleafe it your Maieftie, this is the day
That was appointed for the combating
Betweene the Armourer and his man, my Lord,
And they are ready when your Grace doth pleafe.
King. Then call them forth, that they may try their rights.

*Enter at one doore the Armourer and his neighbours, drinking to him
fo much that he is drunken, and he enters with a drum before him,
and his ftaffe with a fandbag faftened to it, and at the other doore
his man with a drum and fandbag, and Prentifes drinking to him.*

1 *Neighbor.* Here neighbour Horner, I drinke to you in a cup
of Sacke ; and feare not neighbor, you fhall do well enough.
2 *Neigh.* And here neighbor, here's a cup of Charneco.
3 *Neigh.* Here's a pot of good double beere, neighbor drinke
and be merry, and feare not your man.
Arm. Let it come, yfaith Ile pledge you all,
And a figge for Peter.
1 *Pren.* Here Peter, I drinke to thee, and be not affraid.
2 *Pren.* Here Peter, here's a pinte of Claret wine for thee.
3 *Pren.* And here's a quart for me, and be merry Peter,
And feare not thy mafter, fight for credit of the Prentifes.
Peter. I thanke you all, but Ile drinke no more:
Heere Robin, and if I dye, heere I giue thee my hammer,
And Will thou fhalt haue my aperne: and heere Tom,

Take

Yorke and Lancaster.

Take all the money that I haue.
O Lord bleffe me I pray God, for I am neuer able to deale with
my mafter, he hath learn'd fo much fence already.

Salis. Come leaue your drinking, and fall to blowes.
Sirra, what's thy name?

Pet. Peter forfooth.

Salf. Peter: what more?

Pet. Thumpe.

Salf. Thumpe, then fee that thou thumpe thy maifter. .

Arm. Here's to thee Neighbour, fill all the pots againe, for
before wee fight, looke you, I will tell you my minde; for I am
come hither as it were of my mans inftigation, to proue my felfe
an honeft man, and Peter a knaue: and fo haue at you Peter with
downright blowes, as Beuis of South-hampton fell vppon Af-
capart.

Pet. Law you now, I told you hee's in his fence already.

Alarmes, Peter hits him on the head and fels him.

Arm. Hold Peter, I confeffe, Treafon, treafon.   *He dies.*

Pet. O God I giue thee praife.   *He kneels downe*

Pren. Ho well done Peter. God faue the King.

King. Go take hence that Traitor from our fight,
For by his death we do perceiue his guilt,
And God in iuftice hath reueal'd to vs
The truth and innocence of this poore fellow,
Which he had thought to haue murthered wrongfully.
Come fellow, follow vs for thy reward.   *Exit omnes.*

Enter Duke Humfrey and his men, in mour-
ning cloakes.

Hum. Sirra, what's a clocke?

Seruing. Almoft ten my Lord.

Hum. Then is that wofull houre hard at hand,
That my poore Lady fhould come by this way,
In fhamefull penance wandering in the ftreets.
Sweet Nell, ill can thy noble minde abrooke
The abiect people gazing on thy face,
With enuious lookes laughing at thy fhame,
That erft did follow thy proud Chariot wheeles,

When

76

80

84
+85-6
+
+87
+88
+89.91
+91-2 *
*
*

+96-7
+100
+101
102

106

108

II. iv.
+5
+
+6
+
+8

10

12

When thou didst ride in triumph through the streetes

Enter Dame Elnor Cobham bare-foote, and a white sheete about her,
with a waxe Candle in her hand, and verses written on her backe &
pind on, and accompanied with the Sheriffes of London, and Sir Iohn
Standly, and Officers, with Bils and Holbards.

Seruing. My gracious Lord, see wher my Lady comes,
Please it your grace, weele take her from the Sheriffes?

Humph. I charge you for your liues stir not a foote,
Nor offer once to draw a weapon heere,
But let them do their office as they should.

Elnor. Come you my Lord to see my open shame?
Ah *Gloster*, now thou dost penance too,
See how the giddy people looke at thee,
Shaking their heads, and pointing at thee heere,
Go get thee gone, and hide thee from their sights,
And in thy pent vp study rue my shame,
And ban thine enemies. Ah mine and thine.

Hum. Ah *Nell*, sweet *Nell*, forget this extreme griefe,
And beare it patiently to ease thy heart.

Elnor. Ah Gloster, teach me to forget my selfe,
For whilst I thinke I am thy wedded wife,
The thought of this doth kill my wofull heart.
The ruthlesse flints do cut my tender feete,
And when I start, the cruell people laugh,
And bids me be aduised how I tread,
And thus with burning Tapor in my hand,
Malde vp in shame, with papers on my backe,
Ah Gloster, can I endure this and liue?
Sometime ile say I am Duke *Humphreys* wife,
And he a Prince, Protector of the land,
But so he rulde, and such a Prince he was,
As he stood by, whilst I his fore-lorne Dutchesse
Was led with shame, and made a laughing stocke,
To euery idle rascald follower.

Humfrey. My louely *Nell*, what wouldst thou haue me do?
Should

Yorke and Lancaster.

Should I attempt to refcue thee from hence,   † 64

I fhould incurre the danger of the law,   † 66

And thy difgrace would not be fhaddowed fo.   † 65

  Elnor. Be thou milde, and ftir not at my difgrace, † 48

Vntill the axe of death hang ore thy head,   †

As fhortly fure it will. For Suffolke he,   † 51

The new made Duke, that may do all in all   † 51

With her that loues him fo, and hates vs all,   † 52

And impious *Yorke*, and *Bewford* that falfe Prieft,   †

Haue all lymde bufhes to betray thy wings,   †

And flye thou how thou canft, they will entangle thee.   † 55

Enter a Herald of Armes.

  Herald. I fummon your Grace vnto his Highnes Parlament,   † 70

holden at S. *Edmonds-Bury*, the firft of the next Momh.   †

  Hum. A Parliament, and our confent neuer craude   †

Therein before.   This is——————   †

Well, we will be there.   *Exit Herald.*   † 73

Mafter Sheriffe, I pray proceede no further againft my   † 74

     Lady, then the courfe of law extends.   *

  Sher. Pleafe it your Grace, my office here doth end,   † 76

And I muft deliuer her to Sir *Iohn Stanly*.   †

To be conducted into the Ifle of Man.   †

  Humfrey. Muft you fir *Iohn*-conduct my Lady?   † 79

  Standly. I my gracious Lord, for fo it is decreed,   *

And I am fo commanded by the King.   † 80

  Humph. I pray you fir *Iohn*, vfe her nere the worfe,   †

In that I intreate you to vfe her well.   † 81

The world may fmile againe, and I may liue   †

To do you fauour, if you do it her,   †

And fo fir *Iohn* farewell.   84

  Elnor. What gone my Lord, and bid not me farewel   †

  Humph. Witneffe my bleeding heart, I cannot ftay to fpeake   †

                   Exit Humfrey and his men.

  Elnor. Then is he gone, is noble Glofter gone,   † 87

And doth Duke *Humfrey* now forfake me too?   *

Then let me hafte from out faire Englands bounds,   *

Come *Standly* come, and let vs hafte away.   † 91

            D 3   *Standly*

Standly. Madam let's go vnto some house heereby,
Where you may shift your selfe before we go.
Einor Ah good sir Iohn, my shame cannot be hid,
Nor put away with casting off my sheete:
But come let vs go, master Sheriffe farewell,
Thou hast but done thy office as thou shouldst.

Exit omnes

Enter to the Parliament.

Enter two Heralds before, then the Duke of Buckingham, the Duke of Suffolke, and then the Duke of Yorke, and the Cardinall of Winche-ster, and then the King and the Queene, and then the Earle of Sa-lisbury, and the Earle of Warwicke.

King. I wonder our Vnkle Gloster stayes so long.
Queene. Can you not see? or will you not perceiue,
How that ambitious Duke doth vse himselfe?
The time hath beene, but now the time is past,
That none so humble as Duke Humfrey was:
But now let one meete him euen in the morne,
When euery one will giue the time of day,
Yet he will neither moue nor speake to vs.
See you not how the Commons follow him
In troopes, crying, God saue the good Duke Humfrey,
Honouring him as if he were their King?
Gloster is no little man in England,
And if he list to stirre commotions,
Tis likely that the people will follow him.
My Lord, if you imagine there is no such thing,
Then let it passe, and call't a Womans feare.
My Lord of Suffolke, Buckingham, and Yorke,
Disproue my allegations if you can,
And by your speeches, if you can reproue me,
I will subscribe and say, I wrong'd the Duke.
Suf. Well hath your Grace foreseene into that Duke,
And if I had beene licenc'd first to speake,
I thinke I should haue told your Graces tale.
Smooth runnes the brooke, vvhereas the streame is deepest.

No,

Yorke and Lancaster.

No, no, my Soueraigne, Gloſter is a man   *56*
Vnſounded yet, and full of deepe deceite.   *57*

      Enter the Duke of Somerſet.

   King. Welcome Lord Somerſet, what newes from France ?   *83*
   Somer. Cold newes my Lord, and this it is.   *
That all your holds and Townes within thoſe Territories   †*84*
Is ouercome my Lord ; all is loſt.   †
   King. Cold newes indeede Lord Somerſet,   †*86*
but Gods will bee done.
   Yorke. Cold newes for me, for I had hope of France,   *87*
Euen as I haue of fertile England.   †*88*

      Enter Duke Humfrey.

   Hum. Pardon my Liege, that I haue ſtaide ſo long.   †*94*
   Suf. Nay Gloſter know, that thou art come too ſoone,
Vnleſſe thou proue more loyall then thou art,   *96*
We do arreſt thee on high Treaſon heere.
   Hum. Why Suffolkes Duke thou ſhalt not ſee me bluſh, †
Nor change my countenance for thine arreſt   †*99*
Whereof I am guilty, who are my accuſers ?   †*103*
   Yorke. Tis thoght my lord your grace took bribes from Fràce, †
And ſtopt the ſoldiers of their pay,   †
Through which his Maieſty hath loſt all France.   †*106*
   Hum. Is it but thought ſo? And who are they that thinke ſo? †*107*
So God me helpe, as I haue watcht the night,   †*110*
Euer intending good for England ſtill,   †*111*
That peny that euer I tooke from France,   †*109.112*
Be brought againſt me at the iudgement day.   †*114*
I neuer rob'd the ſoldiers of their pay,   *108*
Many a pound of mine owne proper coſt   †*115*
Haue I ſent ouer for the ſoldiers wants,   †*117*
Becauſe I would not racke the needie Commons.   †*116*
   Car. In your Protectorſhip you did deuiſe   .*121*
Strange torments for offenders, by which meanes   †
England hath beene defam'd by tyrannie.   †
   Hum. Why tis well knowne, that whilſt I was Protector. †*124*
Pitty was all the fault that was in me :   _125_
A murtherer or foule felonious Theefe,   †*128-9*

                     That

The contention of the two famous Houses,

† 129
†131-2
†
† 134
† 136
†
†
*
140
142
† 148
† 151
†
† 152
† 155
† 154
† 156
† 158
† 159
† 163
† 161
† 162
† 168
† 167
† 170
171
† 178
†
† 180
182
† 184
† 186
†
† 188

That robs and murders silly passengers,
I torturd aboue the rate of common law.
  Suff. Tush my Lord, these be things of no account,
But greater matters are laid vnto your charge,
I do arrest thee on high treason heere,
And commit thee to my good Lord Cardinall,
Vntill such time as thou canst cleare thy selfe.
  King. Good vnckle obey to his arrest,
I haue no doubt but thou shalt cleare thy selfe,
My conscience tels me thou art innocent.
  Hum. Ah gracious *Henry,* these dayes are dangerous
And would my death might end these miseries,
And stay their moodes for good King *Henries* sake,
But I am made the Prologue to their play,
And thousands more must follow after me.
That dreads not yet their liues destruction.
Suffolkes hatefull tongue blabs his hearts malice,
Bewfords fiery eyes shewes his enuious minde,
Buckinghams proud lookes bewraies his cruel thoghts,
And dogged *Yorke* that leuels at the Moone,
Whose ouerweening arme I haue held backe.
All you haue ioyn'd to betray me thus:
And you my gracious Lady and soueraigne Mistresse,
Causlesse haue laid complaints vpon my head,
I shall not want false witnesses enough,
That so amongst you, you may haue my life.
The Prouerbe no doubt will be perform'd,
A staffe is quickly found to beate a dog.
  Suff. Doth he not twit our soueraigne Lady here,
As if that she with ignominious wrong,
Had suborn'd or hired some to sweare against his life.
  Qu. But I can giue the loser leaue to speake.
  Hum. Far truer spoke then meant, I lose indeed,
Beshrew the winners hearts, they play me false
  Buck. Heele wrest the sence, and keepe vs here al day
My Lord of Winchester, see him sent away.
  Car. Who's within there? Take in Duke Humfrey,

                                                      And

Yorke and Lancaster.

And fee him garded fure within my houfe.

*Hum.*Oh,thus King *Henry* cafts away his crouch, †

Before his legs can beare his body vp, †

And puts his watchfull fhepheard from his fide, †

Whilft wolues ftand fnarring who fhall bite him firft, † 192

Farwell my foueraigne,long maift thou enioy *

Thy fathers happy daies,free from annoy. †

Exit Humfrey with the Cardinals men.

*King.*My Lords,what to your wifdoms fhal feem beft †

Do and vndo as if our felfe were heere. † 196

*Qu.*What,wil your highneffe leaue the Parlament? †

*King.*I *Margaret,*My heart is kild with griefe, † 198

Wheere I may fit and figh in endleffe mone, † 221

For who's a Traitor,Glofter he is none. † 222

Exit King,Salisbury and Warwicke.

*Qu.*Then fit we downe againe my Lord Cardinall, *

Suffolke, Buckingham,Yorke and *Somerfet.* *

Let vs confult of proud Duke *Humfries* fall, *

In mine opinion it were good he dide, † 232

For fafety of our King and Common-wealth. *(211)

*Suf.*And fo thinke I Madam,for as you know, † 252

If our King *Henry* had fhooke hands with death, *

Duke Humfrey then would looke to be our King: † 260

And it may be by pollicie he workes, *

To bring to paffe the thing which now we doubt, *

The Foxe barkes not when he would fteale the Lamb, † 252

But if we take him ere he do the deed, *

We fhould not queftion if that he fhould liue. *

Yorke No,let him die,in that he is a Fox, 251

Leaft that in liuing he offend vs more. *

*Car.*Then let him die before the Commons know, † 240

For feare that they do rife in armes for him. †

*Yorke.*Then do it fodainly my Lords. *

*Suff.*Let that be my Lord Cardinals charge & mine. *(246)

*Car.*Agreed,for hee's already kept within my houfe. *

Enter a Meffenger.

*Qu.*How now firrha,what newes? *

B   *Meffen.*

† 282   *Meſſen.*Madame, I bring you newes from *Ireland*,

† 282-3   The wilde Onele my Lords, is vp in armes,

*   With troupes of Iriſh Kernes, that vncontrolde

*   Doth plant themſelues within the Engliſh pale.

*   And burnes and ſpoiles the Country as they go.

† 289   *Qu.*What redreſſe ſhall we haue for this, My Lords?

†   *Yorke.*'Twere good that my Lord of *Somerſet*

† 291   That fortunate Champion were ſent ouer,

*   To keepe in awe the ſtubborne Iriſhmen,

† 292   He did ſo much good when he was in France.

†   *Somer.*Had *Yorke* bene there with all his farre fetcht

† 293-4 Pollicies, he might haue loſt as much as I.

† 297   *Yorke.*I, for Yorke would haue loſt his life, before

*   That France ſhould haue reuolted from Englands rule.

† 306   *Somer.*I ſo thou mightſt, and yet haue gouern'd worſe then

† 307   *Yorke.*What, worſe then naught? then a ſhame take all,

† 308   *Somer.*Shame on thy ſelfe, that wiſheth ſhame.

304   *Queen.*Somerſet forbeare, good Yorke be patient,

† 312, 318 And do thou take in hand to croſſe the ſeas,

*   With troupes of armed men, to quell the pride

† 314   Of thoſe ambitious Iriſh that rebell.

*   *Yorke.*Well Madame, ſith your Grace is ſo content,

*   Let me haue ſome bandes of choſen ſoldiers,

† 318   And Yorke ſhall trie his fortunes 'gainſt thoſe Kernes.

† 318   *Queen.*Yorke thou ſhalt. My Lord of *Buckingham*,

† 319   Let it be it your charge to muſter vp ſuch ſoldiers

*   As ſhall ſuffice him in theſe needfull warres.

† 315   *Buck.*Madame I will, and leuie ſuch a band.

*   As ſoone ſhall ouercome thoſe Iriſh Rebels.

† 321   But Yorke, where ſhall thoſe Soldiors ſtay for thee?

† 328   *Yorke.*At Briſtow, I'le expect them ten daies hence.

*   *Buck.*Then thither ſhall they come, and ſo farwell.

                                  Exit Buck.

*   *Yorke.*Adieu my Lord of Buckingham.

† 326   *Queen.*Suffolke, remember what you haue to do,

† 322   And you Lord Cardinall, conceming Duke *Humfrey.*

*   T'were good that you did ſee to it in time,

Torke and Lancaster.
Come let vs go,that it may be perform'd.

Exit omnes, Manet Yorke.

Torke. Now Yorke bethinke thy felfe,and rouze thee vp,
Take time whilſt it is offered thee ſo faire,
Leaſt when thou wouldſt,thou canſt it not attaine,
T'was men I lackt,and now they giue them me,
And now whilſt I am buſie in Ireland,
I haue ſeduc'd a head-ſtrong Kentiſhman,
Iohn Cade of *Aſhford,*
Vnder the title of *Iohn Mortimer,*
(For he is like him euery kinde of way)
To raiſe commotion,and by that meanes
I ſhall perceiue how the common people
Do affect the claime and houſe of Yorke,
Then if he haue ſucceſſe in his affaires,
From Ireland then comes Yorke againe,
To reape the harueſt which that coyſtrill ſowed,
Now if he ſhould be taken and condemn'd,
Hee'l nere confeſſe that I did ſet him on,
And therefore ere I go ile ſend him word,
To put in practiſe and to gather head,
That ſo ſoone as I am gone he may begin
To riſe in armes with troopes of country ſwaines,
To helpe him to performe this enterprize.
And then Duke *Humfrey*,be well made away,
None then can ſtop the light to Englands Crowne,
But Yorke can tame, and headlong pull them downe.

Exit Torke.

Then the Curtaines being drawne, Duke Humfrey is diſcouered in his
bed and two men lying on his breſt, and ſmothering him in his bed.
And then enter the Duke of Suffolke to them.

Suff. How now ſirs, what haue you diſpatcht him?
One I my Lord,hee's dead I warrant you.
Suff. Then ſee the cloathes laid ſmoothe about him ſtill,
That when the King comes,he may perceiue
No other,but that he dide of his owne accord.

E 2   2. All

+ 331
*
*
+ 343
+ 348
356
357
349
* (373)
+ 358
+ 374
+ 375
* (379)
+ 380
+ 381
+ 376
+ 378
*
*
*
*
*
+ 382
*
*

III.ii.

+ 6
+ 7
+ 11
+ 10
*

The contention of the two famous Houses,

2. All things is handſome now my Lord.

Suf. Then draw the Curtaines againe and get you gon,
And you ſhall haue your firme reward anon.

Exit murtherers.

*Enter the King and Queene, the Duke of Buckingham, and the Duke
of Somerſet, and the Cardinall.*

†15   *King.* My Lord of Suffolke go call our Vnkle Gloſter,
†   Tell him this day we will that he do cleere himſelfe.
†   *Suffolke.* I will my Lord.   *Exit Saffolke.*
†19-20   *K.* And good my Lords proceed no further 'gainſt our vnckle,
†21   Then by iuſt proofe you can affirme :
†III.i.71   For as the ſucking childe or harmleſſe Lambe,
†III.i.69-70   So is he innocent of treaſon to our State.

Enter Suffolke.

†28   How now Suffolke, where's our Vnckle ?
†29   *Suf.* Dead in his bed, my Lord of Gloſters dead.

The King fals in a ſound.

†33   *Queene.* Aye me, the King is dead : helpe, helpe, my Lords.
†38   *Suf.* Comfort my Lord, gracious *Henry* comfort.
†   *King.* What doth my Lord of Suffolke bid me comfort ?
†40   Came he euen now to ſing a Rauens note,
42   And thinkes he that the cherping of a Wren,
†   By crying comfort through a hollow voyce,
†44   Can ſatisfie my greefes, or eaſe my heart ?
48   Thou balefull meſſenger out of my ſight,
†49   For euen in thine eye-bals murther ſits :
†52   Yet do not goe. Come Baſiliske
†53   And kill the gazer with thy lookes.
56   *Queen.* Why do you rate my Lord of Suffolke thus,
†57   As if that he had cauſd Duke *Humfries* death ?
†66   The Duke and I too you know were enemies,
*(67)   And y'had beſt ſay that I did murther him.
†72   *King.* Ah woe is me for wretched Gloſters death.
†   *Qu.* Be woe for me more wretched then he was :
    What doſt thou turne away and hide thy face ?
75   I am no loathſome Leaper, looke on me.
†82   Was I for this nigh wrackt vpon the ſea,

And

of Yorke and Lancaster.

And thrice by aukward winds driuen back frō Englāds bounds?
What might it bode, but that well foretelling
Winds said, Seeke not a scorpions nest.

Enter the Earles of Warwicke & Salisbury.

War. My Lord, The Commons like an hungry hiue of Bees,
Run vp and downe, caring not whom they sting,
For good Duke *Humfries* death, whom they report
To be murthered by Suffolke and the Cardinall heere.

King. That he is dead good Warwicke, is too true,
But how he dyed God knowes, not *Henry.*

War. Enter his priuy chamber my Lord, and view the body.
Good father stay you with the rude multitude, till I returne.

Salisb. I will sonne.   *Exit Salisbury*

Warwicke drawes the Curtaines, and shewes Duke Hum-
frey in his bed.

King. Ah Vnkle Gloster, heauen receiue thy soule,
Farewell poore *Henries* ioy now thou art gone.

War. Now by his soule that tooke our shape vpon him,
To free vs from his Fathers dreadfull curse,
I am resolu'd that violent hands were laide
Vpon the life of this thrice famous Duke.

Suf. A dreadfull oath, sworne with a solemne tongue,
What instance giues Lord *Warwicke* for these words ?

War. Oft haue I seene a timely parted Ghost,
Of ashy semblance, pale and bloodlesse;
But loe the blood is setled in his face,
More better coloured then when he liu'd.
His well proportion'd beard made rough and sterne,
His fingers spred abroad as one that graspt for life,
Yet was by strength surpris'd, the least of these are probable,
It cannot choose but he was murthered.

Qu. Suffolke, and the Cardinall had him in charge,
And they I trust sir, are no murtherers.

War. I, but tis well knowne they were not his friends,
And tis well seene he found some enemies.

Card. But haue ye no greater proofes then these ?

War. Who sees a heyfer dead and bleeding fresh,

E 3   And

And sees hard by a butcher with an Axe,
But will suspect twas he that made the slaughter?
Who finds the Partridge in the puttockes nest,
But will imagine how the bird came there,
Although the Kyte sore with vnbloudy beake?
Euen so suspitious is this Tragedy.

   Qu. Are you the Kyte *Bewford*, where's his talents?
Is *Suffolke* the butcher, where's his knife?

   Suffolke. I wear no knife to slaughter sleeping men,
Yet here's a vengefull sword rusted with ease,
That shall be scoured in his rancorous heart,
That slanders me with murthers Crimson badge,
Say if thou dare, proud Lord of Warwickshire,
That I am guilty in Duke *Humfries* death.

                       Exit Cardinal

   War. What dares not *Warwicke*, if false *Suffolke* dare him?

   Qu. He dares not calme his contumellious spirit,
Nor cease to be an arrogant controller,
Though *Suffolke* dare him twenty hundred times.

   War. Madam be still, with reuerence may I say it,
That euery word you speake in his defence,
Is slander to your royall Maiesty.

   Suf. Blunt witted Lord, ignoble in thy words,
If euer Lady wrong'd her Lord so much,
Thy mother tooke vnto her blamefull bed,
Some sterne vntutor'd Churle, and Noble stocke
Was graft with Crab-tree slip, whose fruite thou art,
And neuer of the Neuels noble race.

   War. But that the guilt of murther bucklers thee,
And I should rob the deathsman of his fee,
Quitting thee thereby of ten thousand shames;
And that my soueraignes presence makes mee mute,
I would false murtherous coward on thy knees,
Make thee craue pardon for thy passed speech,
And say it was thy mother that thou meantst:
That thou thy selfe was borne in bastardy,
And after all this fearefull homage done,

of Yorke and Lancaster.

Giue thee thy hire, and send thee downe to hell,
Pernitious blood-sucker of sleeping men.

Suf. Thou shouldst be waking whilst I shed thy blood,
If from this presence thou dare go with mee.

War. Away euen now, or I will drag thee hence.

Warwicke puls him out.

*Exit Warwicke and Suffolke, and then all the Commons within, cries,
downe with Suffolke, downe with Suffolke. And then enter againe,
the Duke of Suffolke and Warwicke, with their weapons drawne.*

King. Why how now Lords?

Suff. The traiterous *Warwicke*, with the men of *Berry*,
Set all vpon me mightie Soueraigne.

*The Commons againe cries, downe with Suffolke, downe with
Suffolke. And then enter from them, the Earle
of Salisburie.*

Salisb. My Lord, the Commons sends you word by me,
That vnlesse false Suffolke here be done to death,
Or banished faire Englands Territories,
That they will erre from your highnesse person:
They say by him the good Duke Humfrey dyed,
They say by him they feare the ruine of the Realme,
And therefore if you loue your subiects weale,
They wish you to banish him from forth the land.

Suf. Indeed tis like the Commons, rude vnpolisht hindes
Would send such message to their Soueraigne:
But you my Lord were glad to be imploy'd,
To try how quaint an Orator you were:
But all the honour Salsbury hath got,
Is, that he was the Lord Embassador,
Sent from a sort of Tinkers to the King.   *The Commons cryes,
an answere from the King my Lord of Salsbury.*

King. Good Salsbury go backe againe to them,
Tell them we thanke them all for their kinde care,
And had I not bene cited thus by their meanes,
My selfe had done it. Therefore heere I sweare,
If Suffolke be found to breathe in any place
Where I haue rule, but three dayes more, he dies. *Exit Salisbury*
                                                    Qu.

Qu. Oh *Henry,* reuerse the doome of gentle Suffolkes banish-
ment.

King. Vngentle Queene to call him gentle *Suffolke,*
Speake not for him, for in England he shall not rest,
If I say, I may relent, but if I sweare, it is irreuocable.
Come good *Warwicke,* and go thou in with me,
For I haue great matters to impart to thee.

    Exit King and Warwicke, Manet Qu. and Suffolke.

Queene. Hell fire and vengeance go along with you,
There's two of you, the diuell make the third,
Fie womanish man, canst thou not curse thy enemies?

   Suff. A plague vpon them, wherefore should I curse them?
Could curses kill as do the Mandrakes grones,
I would inuent as many bitter termes,
Deliuered strongly through my fixed teeth,
With twice so mauy signes of deadly hate,
As leane fac'd enuy in her loathsome caue.
My tongue should stumble in mine earnest words,
Mine eyes should sparkle like the beaten flint,
My haire be fixt on end, as one distraught,
And euery ioynt should seeme to curse and ban,
And now me-thinkes my burthened heart would breake,
Should I not curse them. Poison be their drinke,
Gall worse then gall, the daintiest thing they taste,
Their sweetest shade a groue of Cypresse trees,
Their softest touch as smart as lyzards stings.
Their musicke frightfull, like the serpents hisse.
And boding scritch-owles make the consort full.
All the foule terrors in darke seated hell.

   Qu. Enough sweete *Suffolke,* thou torments thy selfe.

   Suff. You bad me ban, and will you bid me cease?
Now by this ground that I am banisht from,
Well could I curse away a winters night,
And standing naked on a Mountaine top,
Where byting cold would neuer let grasse grow,
And thinke it but a minute spent in sport.

                               Queene

Yorke and Lancaster.

*Queene.*No more.Sweete *Suffolke* hie thee hence to *France*,
Or liue where thou wilt within this worlds globe,
Ile haue an Irish that shalt finde thee out,
And long thou shalt not stay,but ile haue thee repeald,
Or venter to be banished my selfe.
Oh let this kisse be printed in thy hand,
That when thou feest it,thou maist thinke on me.
Away I say,that I may feele my griefe,
For it is nothing whilst thou standest heere.

*Suffolke.*Thus is poore *Suffolke* ten times banished,
Once by the King,but three times thrice by thee.

Enter Vawse.

*Queene.*How now,whither goes *Vawse* so fast ?

*Vawse.*To signifie vnto his Maiesty,
That Cardinall *Beuford* is at point of death,
Sometimes he raues and cries as he were mad,
Sometimes he cals vpon Duke *Humfries* Ghost,
And whispers to his Pillow as to him,
And sometimes he cals to speake vnto the King,
And I am going to certifie vnto his Grace,
That euen now he cald aloud for him.

Queene. Go then good *Vawse* and certifie the King.

Exit Vawse.

Oh what is worldly pompe,all men must die,
And woe am I for *Beufords* heauy end.
But why mourne I for him,whilst thou art heere?
Sweete *Suffolke* hie thee hence to France,
For if the King do come,thou sure must die.

*Suff.*And if I go I cannot liue : but heere to die,
VVhat were it else,but like a pleasant slumber in thy lap ?
Heere could I breathe my soule into the ayre,
as milde and gentle as the new borne babe,
That dies with mothers dug betweene his lips,
VVhere from my sight I should be raging madde,
and call for thee to close mine eyes,
Or with thy lips to stop my dying soule,
That I might breathe it so into thy body,

F   and

+405
+406
407
+349
+350
+343
+344
+346
+347
357
+358
+367
369
*
+373
375
+374
+377
+
+379
+380
•
+381
+386,405
+386-7
+388
+389 90
+392
+
-395
+
-398

And then it liu'd in sweete Elyziam,
By thee to die,were but to dye in ieast,
From thee to dye,were torment more then death,
Oh,let me stay,befall what may befall.

 *Queene.*Oh might st thou stay with safety of thy life,
Then shonldst thou stay,but heauens deny It,
And therefore go,but hope ere long to be repeald.

 *Suff.*I goe.

 *Queene.*And take my heart with thee.

      She kisseth him.

 *Suff.*A iewell lockt into the wofulst caske,
That euer yet containd a thing of worth.
Thus like a splitted Barke,so sunder we,
This way fall I to death.   *Exit Suffolke.*

 *Queene.*This way for me.   *Exit Queene.*

*Enter King and Salisbury,and then the Curtaines be drawne, and the
 Cardinall is discouered in his bed, rauing and staring as if he were
 mad.*

 *Car.*Oh death, if thou wilt let me liue but one whole yeare,
I'le giue thee as much gold as will purchase such another Island.

 *King.*Oh,seeing Lord of Salisbury how he is troubled,
Lord Cardinall,remember Christ must saue thy soule.

 Car. Why died he not in his bed?
What would you haue me to do then?
Can I make men liue whether they will or no?
Sirra,go fetch me the poyson which the Pothicary sent me.
Oh, see where Duke *Humfries* ghost doth stand,
And stares me in the face.Looke,looke,coame downe his haire,
So now hee's gone againe: Oh,oh,oh.

 *Sal.*See how the pangs of death doth gripe his heart.

 *King.*Lord Cardinall if thou diest assured of heauenly blisse,
Hold vp thy hand and make some signe to vs. *Car.dies.*
Oh see he dyes,and makes no signe at all,
Oh God forgiue his soule.

 *Sal.*So bad an end did neuer none behold,
But as his death,so was his life in all.

                King

Yorke and Lancaster.

*King.*Forbeare to iudge, good Salsbury forbeare,
For God will iudge vs all.
Go take him hence, and see his funerals perform'd.

Exitomnes.

Alarmes within, and the Chambers bee discharged, like as it were a
fight at sea. And then enter the Captaine of the ship, and the Ma-
ster, and the Masters mate, and the Duke of Suffolke disguised, and
others with him, & Water Whickmore.

*Cap.*Bring forward these prisoners that scorn'd to yeeld,
Vnlade their goods with speed, and sincke their ship,
Here Master, this prisoner I giue to you.
This other, the Masters mate shall haue,
And *Water Whickmore* thou shalt haue this man,
And let them pay their ransome ere they passe.
Suffolke. Water!   *He starteth.*
*Water.*How now, what dost feare me?
Thou shalt haue better cause anon.
*Suff.*It is thy name affrights me, not thy selfe.
I do remember well, a cunning wizzard told me,
That by Water I should dye:
Yet let not that make thee bloody minded,
Thy name being rightly sounded,
Is *Gualter*, not *Walter*.
*Walter.*Gualter or Water, al's one to me,
I am the man must bring thee to thy death.
*Suff.*I am a Gentleman, looke on my Ring,
Ransome me at what thou wilt, it shall be paid.
*Water.*I lost mine eye in boording of the ship,
And therefore ere I Merchant-like sell blood for gold,
Then cast me headlong downe into the sea.
*2. Prison,*But what shall our ransomes be?
*Mai.*A hundred pounds a peece eyther pay that or dye.
*2. Prison.*Then saue our liues, it shall be paide.
*Water.*Come sirra, thy life shall be the ransome I wil haue.
*Suff.*Stay villaine, thy prisoner is a Prince,

F 2   The

The Duke of Suffolke, *William de la Pole.*

Cap. The Duke of Suffolke folded vp in rags.

Suff. I sir, but these rags are no part of the Duke,
Ioue sometime went disguisde, and why not I?

Cap. I, but *Ioue* was neuer slaine as thou shalt be

Suff. Base lady groome, King *Henries* blood,
The honourable blood of *Lancaster,*
Cannot be shed by such a lowly swaine,
I am sent ambassador for the Queene to France,
I charge thee waffe me crosse the channell safe.

Cap. Ile waffe thee to thy death, go Water take him hence,
And on our long boates side, chop off his head.

Suff. Thou dar'st not for thine owne.

Cap. Yes *Pole.*

Suffolke. Pole.

Cap. I *Pole,* puddle, kennell, sinke and durt,
Ile stop that yawning mouth of thine,
Those lips of thine that so oft haue kist the
Queene, shall sweepe the ground, and thou that
Smild'st at good Duke *Humfries* death,
Shalt liue no longer to infect the earth.

Suffolke. This villaine being but Captaine of a Pinnis,
Threatens more plagues then mighty *Abradas,*
The great *Macedonian* Pyrate,
Thy words addes fury and not remorse in me.

Cap. I but my deeds shall stay thy fury soone.

Suffolke. Hast not thou waited at my Trencher,
When we haue feasted with Queene *Margaret?*
Hast not thou kist thy hand, and held my stirrop?
and bare-head plodded by my footclooth Mule,
and thought thee happy when I smilde on thee?
This hand hath writ in thy defence,
Then shall I charme thee, hold thy lauish tongue.

Cap. Away with him *Water,* I say, and off with his head.

1. Prison. Good my Lord, entreate him mildly for your life.

Suff. First let this necke stoupe to the axes edge,
Before this knee do bow to any,

Yorke and Lancaster.

Saue to the God of heauen, and to my King :
Suffolkes imperiall tongue cannot plead
To such a ladie groome.

Water. Come, come, why do we let him speake ?
I long to haue his head for ransome of mine eye.

Suff: A Swordar and Bandetto slaue
Murthered sweete Tully,
Brutus bastard hand stabd Iulius Cæsar,
And Suffolke dyes by Pirates on the seas.

Exit Suffolke and Water.

Cap. Off with his head, and send it to the Queene,
And ransomlesse this prisoner shall go free,
To see it safe deliuered vnto her.
Come lets go. *Exit omnes.*

Enter two of the Rebels with long staues.

George. Come away Nicke, and put a long staffe in thy pike, &
prouide thy selfe, for I can tell thee, they haue bene vp this two
dayes.

Nicke. Then they had more neede to go to bed now,
But sirra George, what's the matter ?

George, Why sirra, Iack Cade the Dier of Ashford heere,
He meanes to turne this land, and set a new nap on't.

Nicke. I marry he had need so, for tis growne thred-bare,
Twas neuer merry world with vs, since these Gentlemen came
vp.

George. I warrant thee thou shalt neuer see a Lord weare a lea-
ther apron now a-daies.

Nicke. But sirra, who comes elfe beside Iacke Cade ?.

George. Why there's Dicke the butcher, and Robin the Sadler,
and Will that came a wooing to our Nan last Sunday, and Harry
and Tom, and Gregory that should haue your Parnill, & a great
fort more is come from Rochester, and from Maidstone & Can-
terbury, and all the townes hereabouts, and we must be al Lords
or Squires, assoone as Iacke Cade is King.

Nicke. Harke, harke, I heare the Drum, they be comming.

Enter Iacke Cade, Dicke Butcher, Robin, Will, Tom,
Harry, and the rest with long staues.

F 3 *Cade.*

45.
122
†121
*(42)
†131
*(26)
†135

†138
†142-3
*(139-40)
*
†141
IV. ii.
†1
·†2

†3-4
*
†5
†6-7
†8
†9-10

*
†13-14
*·
†27
*
*
*
*
*
*
{
†

The contention of the two famous Houses,

†39   *Cade.* Proclaime silence.

40   *All.* Silence.

†34   *Cade.* I Iohn Cade, so named for my valiancy.

†35-6   *Dicke.* Or rather for stealing of a cade of sprats.

41   *Cade.* My father, was a Mortimer.

42   *Dicke.* He was an honest man, and a good bricke-layer.

†44   *Cade.* My mother came of the Lacies.

†48-9   *Nicke.* She was a Pedlers daughter indeed, & sold many laces.

†50-1   *Robin.* And now being not able to occupy her furr'd packe,

†51-2   She washeth buckes vp and downe the countrey.

†   *Cade.* Therefore I am honourably borne.

†   *Harry.* I the field is honourable, for hee was borne vnder a

†56   hedge, because his father had no other house but the cage.

60   *Cade.* I am able to endure much.

†   *George.* That's true, I know he can endure any thing,

†61-2   For I haue seene him whipt two market dayes togither.

   Cadr. I feare neither sword nor fire.

64-5   *Will.* He neede not feare the sword, for his coate is of proofe.

†   *Dicke.* But methinkes he should feare the fire, being so often

67-8   burnt in the hand, for stealing of sheepe.

†   *Cade.* Therefore be braue, for your Captain is braue, & vowes

†   reformation : you shall haue seuen halfepeny loaues for a penny,

†72   and the three hoopt pot shall haue ten hoopes, and it shalbe fel-

†75-6   lony to drinke small beere, if I be King, as King I will be.

†77-9   *All.* God saue your Maiesty.

†80   *Cade.* I thanke you good people, you shall all eate and drinke

(IV.vii.38)*   of my score, and go all in my liuery ; and wee'll haue no writing

†IV.vii.7   but the score and the Tally, and there shall be no lawes but such

   as come from my mouth.

†IV.vii.9-10   *Dicke.* Wee shall haue sore lawes then, for he was thrust into

†   the mouth the other day.

†IV.vii.12-13   *Geo.* I and stinking law too, for his breath stinkes so, that one

*   cannot abide it.

   Enter Will with the Clarke of Chattam.

^   *Will.* Oh Captaine, a prize.

†91   *Cade.* Who's that *Will* ?

92-3   *Will,* The Clarke of Chattam, he can write and reade and cast

   account,

account, I tooke him setting of boyes copies, and he has a book in his pocket with red letters.

Cade. Zounds he's a Coniurer, bring him hither, Now sir, what's your name?

Clarke. Emanuell sir, and it shall please ye.

Dicke. It will go hard with you I tell ye, For they vse to write that ore the top of Letters.

Cade. What do ye vse to write your name? Or do you as ancient forefathers haue done, vse the score and the Tally?

Clarke. Nay truly sir, I praise God I haue bene so wel broght vp, that I can write mine owne name.

Cade. Oh he has confest, go hang him with his pen and inkehorne about his necke. *Exit one with the Clarke.*

Enter Tom.

Tom. Captaine, Newes, newes, sir *Humfrey Stafford* and his brother are coming with the Kings power, & mean to kil vs all.

Cade. Let them come, he's but a Knight is he?

Tom. No, no, he's but a Knight.

Cade. Why then to equall him, Ile make my selfe Knight. Kneele downe Iohn Mortemer, Rise vp sir Iohn Mortemer. Is there any more of them that be Knights?

Tom. I his brother.

Cade. Then kneele downe Dicke Butcher.

He knights him.

Rise vp sir Dicke Butcher. Now sound vp the drum.

Enter Sir Humfrey Stafford and his Brother, with Drum and Soldiers.

Cade. As for these silken coated slaues, I passe not a pin, Tis to you good people that I speake.

Staf. Why Country-men, what meane you thus in troopes, To follow this rebellious Traitor Cade? Why his Father was a brick-layer.

Cade. Well, and Adam was a Gardiner, what then? But I come of the Mortemers.

Staf. I, the Duke of Yorke hath taught you that.

Cade

The contention of the two famous Houses,

Cade. The Duke of Yorke, nay I learnt it my selfe,

For looke you, *Roger Mortimer* the Earle of March,

Married the Duke of Clarence daughter.

    Staf. Well, that's true: But what then ≀

    Cade. And by her he had two children at a birth.

    Staf. That's false.

    Cade. I, but I say tis true.

    All. Why then tis true.

    Cade. And one of them was stolne away by a begger-woman,

And that was my father, and I am his sonne,

Deny it and you can.

    Nicke. Nay looke you, I know was true;

For his father built a chimney in my fathers house,

And the brickes are aliue at this day to testifye it.

    Cade. But doest thou heare Stafford, tell the King, that for his

fathers sake, in whose time boyes playde at span-counter with

French Crownes, I am content that he shall be King as long as

he liues : marry alwaies prouided, Ile be Protector ouer him.

    Staf. O monstrous simplicity.

    Cade. And tell him, wee'll haue the Lord *Sayes* head, and the

Duke of Somersets, for deliuering vp the Dukedomes of *Aniey*

and *Mayne,* and selling the Townes in France: by which means

England hath bene maim'd euer since, and gone as it were with a

crutch, but that my puissance held it vp. And besides, they can

speake French, and therefore they are Traitors,

    Staf. As how I prethee ?

    Cade. Why the Frenchmen are our enemies, be they not ?

And then can he that speakes with the tongue of an enemy be a

good subiect ? Answere me to that.

    Staf. Well sirra, wilt thou yeeld thy selfe vnto the Kings mer-

cy, and he wil pardon thee and these, their outrages and rebelli-

ous deeds ?

    Cade. Nay, bid the King come to me and he will, and then Ile

pardon him, or otherwaies ile haue his Crowne tell him, ere it

be long.

    Staf. Go Herald, proclaime in all the Kings Townes,

That those that will forsake the Rebell Cade,

Shall

+ 143
+ 144
+ 145
*(146)
+ 147

+ 149
*
+ 150-1
+ 154
+
+ 155
+
+ 157-8
+ 164
+
+
+ 167-8
*(178)
+169-70
+ 170
+ 172
+ 172
+ 173
+ 176-7
*
+ 179-80
+ 180-1
+ 182
*
*
*
*
*
*
+ 186
+ 187

Yorke and Lancaster.

Shall haue free pardon from his Maiesty.

Exit Stafford and h is men.

Cade. Come firs, S. George for vs and Kent.   *Exit omnes.*

Alarmes to the battell, where sir Humfrey Stafford and his brother
are both slaine. Then enters Iacke Cade
againe, and the rest.

Cade. Sir Dicke Butcher, thou hast fought to day most valiantly, and knockt them down as if thou hadst bin in thy slaugh-
ter-house, and thus I will reward thee : The Lent shall bee as
long againe as it was, and thou shalt haue licenfe to kil for four-
score and one a weeke. Drum strike vp, for now weel march to
London, and to morrow I mean to sit in the Kings seat at Westminster.   *Exit omnes*

Enter the King reading of a Letter, and the Queene with the
Duke of Suffolkes head, and the Lord Say,
with others.

King. Sir *Humphrey Stafford* and his brother is slaine,
And the Rebels march amaine to London.
Go backe to them, and tell them thus from me,
Ile come and parley with their Generall.
Yet stay, Ile reade the Letter once againe ;
Lord Say, Iacke Cade hath solemnly vow'd to haue thy head.

Say. I, but I hope your highnesse shall haue his.

King. How now Madam, still lamenting and mourning for
Suffolkes death ? I feare my Loue if I had bin dead, thou woldst
not haue mourn'd so much for me.

Qu. No my loue, I should not mourne, but dye for thee.

Enter a Messenger.

Mes. Oh flye my Lord, the Rebels are entred Southwarke,
And haue almost wonne the Bridge,
Calling your Grace an vsurper :
And that monstrous Rebell Cade, hath sworne
To crowne himselfe King in Westminster,
Therefore flye my Lord, and post to Killingworth.

King. Go bid Buckingham and Clifford, gather
An army vp, and meete with the Rebels.

G   Come

IV. iv.

†34

†1
†6
†7
†8
†20

†34

†13
†14
†19
20

†23
24
25

†27

†30
†28
†31
†39

Come Madame, let vs haſte to Killingworth.
Come on Lord Say,go thou along with vs,
For feare the Rebell Cade do finde thee out.

Say. My innocence my Lord ſhall pleade for me,
And therefore with your highneſſe leaue,Ile ſtay behind.

*King.*Euen as thou wilt my Lord Say :
Come Madam. let vs go.　　　　　　　*Exit omnes*

*Enter the Sord Skayles vpon the Tower
walles walking.*

L.Skayles. How now, is Iacke Cade ſlaine ?
1.Cit. No my Lord, nor likely to be ſlaine,
For they haue worme the bridge,
Killing all thoſe that withſtand them.
The Lord Mayor craueth aide of your honor from the Tower,
To defend the City from the Rebels.

Lord Ska. Such aide as I can ſpare, you ſhall command,
But I am troubled heere with them my ſelfe,
The Rebels haue attempted to win the Tower,
But get you to Smithfield and gather head,
And thither will I ſend you Mathew Goffe :
Fight for your King, your Countrey,and your liues,
And ſo farewell,for I muſt hence againe.

　　　　　　　　　　　　　　　Exit omnes.
*Enter Iacke Cade, and the reſt, and ſtrikes his ſword vpon
London ſtone.*

Cade. Now is Mortemer Lord of this City,
And now ſitting vpon London ſtone, We command,
That the firſt yeare of our reigne,
The piſſing Cundit run nothing but red wine.
And now henceforward, it ſhall bee treaſon
For any that calles me any otherwiſe then
Lord Mortemer.

　　　　　　　　Enter a ſouldier.
Soul. Iacke Cade,Iacke Cade.
Cade. Zounds knocke him downe.　　　*They kil him*
Dicke. My Lord,

　　　　　　　　　　　　　　　　　Ther's

Ther's an Army gathered together into Smithfield.

   Cade. Come then, let's go fight with them,
But firft go on and fet London-bridge a fire,
And if you can, burne downe the Tower too.
Come let's away.   *Exit omnes*

Alarmes, and then Mathew Goffe is flaine, and all the reft
with him. Then enter Iacke Cade a-
gaine and his company.

   Cade. So firs, now go and pull downe the Sauoy,
Others to the Innes of Court, downe with them all.

   Dick. I haue a fute vnto your Lordfhip.

   Cade. Be it a Lordfhip Dicke, and thou fhalt haue it
For that word.

   Dicke. That we may go burne all the Records,
And that all writing may be put downe,
And nothing vfed but the fcore and Tally.

   Cade. Dicke it fhall be fo, and henceforward all things fhall
be in common,
And in Cheapfide fhall my palphrey go to graffe.
Why ift not a miferable thing, that of the skin of an innocent
Lambe parchment fhould be made,& then with a little blotting
ouer with inke, a man fhould vndo himfelfe.

   Some faies tis the bees that fting, but I fay tis their waxe, for
I am fure I neuer feal'd to any thing but once, and I was neuer
mine owne man fince.

   Nick. But when fhall we take vp thofe commodities
Which you told vs of.

   Cade. Marry he that will luftily ftand to it, fhall take vp thefe
commodities following: Item, a gown, a kirtle, a petticoat, and
a fmocke.   *Enter George.*

   Geor. My Lord, a prize, a prize, heres the Lord Say,
Which fold the Townes in France.

   Cade. Come hither thou Say, thou George, thou Buckrum
Lord, What anfwer canft thou make vnto my mightineffe, for
deliuering vp the Townes in France to Mounfier bus mine cue,
the Dolphin of France?

And more then ſo, thou haſt moſt traitorouſly erected a Gram-
mar ſchoole, to infect the youth of the Realme, and againſt the
Kings Crowne and dignity, thou haſt built vp a paper Mill; nay
it will bee ſaide to thy face, that thou keep'ſt men in thy houſe
that daily reads of bookes with red letters, & talks of a Nowne
and a Verbe, and ſuch abhominable words as no Chriſtian eare
is able to endure it.

And beſides all this, thou haſt appointed certaine Iuſtices of
the Peace, in euery ſhire, to hang honeſt men that ſteal for their
liuing, and becauſe they could not reade, thou haſt hung them
vp : onely for which cauſe, they were moſt worthy to liue.
Thou rideſt on a foot-cloth, doſt thou not ?

Say. Yes, what of that ?

Cade. Marry I ſay, thou oughteſt not to let thy horſe weare a
cloake, when an honeſter man then thy ſelfe, goes in his hoſe &
doublet.

Say. You men of Kent.

All. Kent, what of Kent ?

Say. Nothing, but *Bona terra.*

Cade. Bonum-terum, zounds what's that ?

Dicke. He ſpeakes French.

Will. No tis Dutch.

Nicke. No tis Outalian, I know it well erough.

Say. Kent (in the Commentaries Cæſar wrote)
Term'd it the ciuilſt place of all this Land :
Then Noble Country-men heare me but ſpeake,
I ſold not France, nor loſt I Normandie.

Cade. But wherefore doſt thou ſhake thy head ſo ?

Say. It is the palſie, and not feare that makes me.

Cade. Nay, thou noddſt thy head at vs, as who wouldſt ſay,
Thou wilt be euen with me if thou getſt away :
But ile make thee ſure enough now I haue thee.
Go take him to the ſtandard in Cheape-ſide, and choppe off his
head, and then go to Mile-end greene to ſir Iames Cromer his
ſon in Law, and cut off his head too, and bring them to me vppon two poles preſently. Away with him.

Exit one or two with the Lord Say.

There

of Yorke and Lancaſter.

There ſhall not a Nobleman weare a head on his ſhoulders.
But he ſhall pay me tribute for it.
Nor there ſhall not a maide be married, but he ſhall fee to mee
for her.
Mayden-head or elſe, lle haue it my ſelfe :
Marry I will that married men ſhall hold of me in *capite*,
And that their wiues ſhall be as free as heart can think, or toong
can tell.

        Enter Robin.

  Rob. O Captaine, London-bridge is a fire.
  Cad. Runne to Billingſgate, and fetch Pitch and Flaxe, and
quench it.

        Enter Dicke and a Sargeant.

  Sargeant. Iuſtice, iuſtice, I pray you ſir, let me haue iuſtice of
this fellow heere.
  Cade. Why what has he done?
  Sarg. Alas ſir he has rauiſht my wife.
  Dick. Why my Lord he would haue reſted me,
And I went and entred my Action in his wiues paper houſe.
  Cade. Dicke follow thy ſute in her common place.
Your horſon villaine, you are a Sergeant, you'l
Take any man by the throate for twelue pence :
And reſt a man when he is at dinner,
And haue him to priſon ere the meate be out on's mouth.
Go Dicke take him hence, and cut out his tongue for cogging,
Hough him for running, and to conclude,
Braue him with his owne mace.

        Exit with the Sargeant.
    Enter two with the Lord Sayes head, and ſir Iames
        Cromers, vpon two poles.

So, come carry them before me, and at euery lanes end, let them
kiſſe together.

    Enter the Duke of Buckingham, and Lord Clifford, the
        Earle of Cumberland.

  Clif. Why Countrey-men, and warlike friends of Kent,
What meanes theſe mutinous rebellions,
That you in troopes do muſter thus your ſelues,

        G 3   Vnder

The contention of the two famous Houses.

Vnder the conduct of this Traitor Cade?
To rise againſt your Soueraigne Lord and King,
Who mildly hath his pardon ſent to you,
If you forſake this monſtrous Rebell heere?
If honor be the marke whereat you ayme,
Then haſt to France that our fore-fathers won,
And win againe that thing which now is loſt,
And leaue to ſeeke your Countries ouerthrow.
 All. A Clifford, a Clifford.

　　　　　　　　　　They forſake Cade

 Cade. Why how now, wil you forſake your general,
And ancient freedome which you haue poſſeſt?
To bend your neckes vnder their ſeruile yokes,
Who if you ſtir, will ſtraight way hang you vp.
But follow me, and you ſhall pull them downe,
And make them yeeld their liuings to your hands.
 All. A Cade, a Cade.

　　　　　　They run to Cade againe.

 Clif. Braue warlike friends, heare me but ſpeake,
Refuſe not good whilſt it is offered you :
The King is mercifull, then yeelde to him,
And I my ſelfe will go along with you
To Winſore Caſtle, whereas the King abides,
And on mine honour you ſhall haue no hurt.
 All. A Clifford, a Clifford, God ſaue the King.
 Cade. How like a feather is this raſcall company
Blowne euery way?
But that they may ſee there wants no valiancy in me,
My ſtaffe ſhall make way through the midſt of you,
And ſo a poxe take you all.

　　　　He runs through them with his ſtaffe,
　　　　　　　and then flies away.

 Buc. Go ſome and make after him, and proclaime,
That thoſe that can bring the head of Cade,
Shall haue a thouſand Crownes for his labour.
Come march away.　　　　　　　　　　*Exit om.*

　　　　　　　　　　　　　　　　　　Enter

of Yorke and Lancaster.

Enter King Henry, and the Queene, and Somerset.

King. Lord Sommerset, what newes heare you of the Rebell Cade?

Som. This my gracious Lord, that the Lord Say is done to death, and the City is almost sackt.

King. Gods will be done, for as he hath decreed, so must it be: And be as he please, to stop the pride of those rebellious men.

Qu. Had the noble Duke of Suffolke bene aliue,
The Rebell Cade had bene supprest ere this,
And all the rest that do take part with him.

Enter the Duke of Buckingham and Clifford, with the Rebels, with halters about their neckes.

Cliff. Long liue King Henry, Englands lawfull King:
Loe heere my Lord, these Rebels are subdude,
And offer their liues before your highnesse feete.

King. But tell me Clifford, is their Captaine heere?

Clif. No my gracious Lord, he is fled away, but proclamations are sent forth, that he that can but bring his head shall haue a thousand crownes. But may it please your Maiesty to pardon these their faults, that by these traitors means were thus misled.

King. Stand vp you simple men, and giue God praise,
For you did take in hand you know not what,
And go in peace obedient to your King,
And liue as subiects, and you shall not want,
Whilst Henry liues, and weares the English Crowne.

All. God saue the King, God saue the King.

King. Come let vs hast to London now with speede,
That solemne processions may be sung,
In laud and honor of the God of heauen,
And triumphs of this happy victorie.   *Exit omnes*

Enter Iacke Cade at one doore, and at the other, M. Alexander Eyden and his men, and Iacke Cade lies down picking of hearbes and eating them.

Eyden. Good Lord how pleasant is this country lite,
This little land my father left me heere,
With my contented minde, serues me as well,
As all the pleasures in the Court can yeeld,

                                        Not

†18
†26
†28
†30
31-2
†33,34
†35
†36
†38
†39
40.1
†
43-4
†
47
†50
†51
*
*
†59-60
†61
†62-3
†64,78
†64
†65-6
†66-7
†69
†71
71
†
†
*
†86
†88-9

The contention of the two famous Houses,

Nor would I change this pleasure for the Court.

Cade. Zounds, heere's the Lord of the foyle : Stand villaine,
thou wilt betray me to the King, and get a thousand Crownes
for my head : but ere thou goeft, ile make thee eate yron like an
Eftridge, and fwallow my fword like a great pin.

Eyden. Why fawcy companion, why fhould I betray thee?
Ift not enough that thou haft broke my hedges,
And enter'd into my ground, without the leaue of me the owner
But thou wilt braue me too.

Cade. Braue thee and beard thee too, by the beft blood of the
Realme. Looke on me well, I haue eate no meat this fiue daies,
yet if do not leaue thee and thy fiue men as dead as a dore naile,
I pray God I may neuer eate graffe more.

Eyden. Nay, it fhall neuer be faid whilft the world ftands,
That *Alexander Eyden* an Efquire of Kent,
Tooke oddes to combate with a famifht man.
Looke on me, my limbes are equall vnto thine,
And euery way as bigge : then hand to hand
Ile combat with thee. Sirra, fetch me weapons,
And ftand you all afide.

Cade. Now fword, if thou doft not hew this burly-bon'd churl
into chines of beefe, I would thou mightft fall into fome Smiths
hand, and be turn'd to hobnailes.

Eyden. Come on thy way.

They fight, and Cade fals downe.

Cade. Oh Villaine, thou haft flaine the flower of Kent for chi-
ualry, but it is famine and not thee that has done it. For come
ten thoufand diuels, and giue me but the ten meales that I wan-
ted this fiue dayes, and ile fight with you all. And fo a poxe rot
thee, for Iacke Cade muft dye. *He dyes.*

Eyden. Iacke Cade : And was this that monftrous rebel which
I haue flaine?
Oh fword, ile honour thee for this, and in my chamber
Shalt thou hang as a monument to after age,
For this great-feruice thou haft done to me.
Ile drag him hence, and with my fword
Cut off his head, and beare it to the King. *Exit.*
Enter

Yorke and Lancaster.

Enter the Duke of Yorke with Drum and Soldiours.

Yorke. In armes from Ireland comes Yorke amaine,
Ring belles aloud, bonfires perfume the ayre,
To entertaine faire Englands royall King.
Ah *Sancta Maiesta*, who would not buy thee deare?

Enter the Duke of Buckingham,

But soft, who comes heere, Buckingham, what newes with him?

Buck. Yorke, if thou meane well, I greete thee so.

Yorke. Humphrey of Buckingham, welcome I sweare:
What, comes thou in loue, or as a Mssenger?

Buck. I come as a Messenger frō our dread Lord & soueraigne,
Henry. To know the reason of these armes in peace?
Or that thou being a subiect as I am,
Shouldst thus approch so neare with colours spread,
Whereas the person of the King doth keepe?

Yorke. A subiect as he is!
Oh how I hate these spitefull abiect tearmes,
But Yorke dissemble, till thou meete thy sonnes,
Who now in Armes expect their fathers sight,
And not farre hence I know they cannot be.
Humfrey Duke of *Buckingham*, pardon me,
That I answer'd not at first, my minde was troubled,
I came to remoue that monstrous rebell *Cade*,
And heaue proud Somerset from out the Court,
That basely yeelded vp the Townes in France.

Buck. Why that was presumption on thy behalfe,
But if it be no otherwise then so,
The King doth pardon thee, and granst to thy request,
And Somerset is sent vnto the Tower.

Yorke. Vpon thine honour is it so?

Buck. Yorke, he is vpon mine honour.

Yorke. Then before thy face, I heere dismisse my troopes,
Sirs, meete me to morrow in Saint *Georges* fields,
And there you shall receiue your pay of me.

Exit Soldiers.

Buck. Come *Yorke*, thou shalt go speake vnto the King,
But see, his grace is comming to meete with vs.

H   *Enter*

† 1
† 3
† 4
† 5
† 12
† 14
†
† 16
†
†
† 19
† 22
*
*
† 25
*
*
*
† 32
† 33-4
† 62
† 61, 36
*
† 38
†
† 40
†
†
†
† 44
† 46
† 47
† 54
† 55

Enter King Henry.

King. How now *Buckingham,* is *Yorke* friends with vs,
That thus thou bringft him in hand with thee ?

Buck. He is my Lord, and hath difcharg'd his troopes,
Which came with him, but as your Grace did fay,
To heaue the Duke of Somerfet from hence,
And to fubdue the Rebels that were vp.

King. Then welcome coufin *Yorke,* giue me thy hand,
And thankes for thy great feruice done to vs,
Againft thofe traiterous Irifh that rebeld.

Enter Mafter Eyden with Iacke Cades head.

Eyden. Long liue King *Henry* in triumphant peace,
Loe heere my Lord vpon my bended knees,
I heere prefent the traiterous head of *Cade,*
That hand to hand in fingle fight I flue.

King. Firft thanks to heauen, and next to thee my friend,
That haft fubdude that wicked traitor thus.
Oh let me fee that head that in his life
Did worke me and my land fuch cruell fpight.
A vifage fterne, cole blacke his curled lockes,
Deepe trenched furrowes in his frowning brow,
Prefageth warlike humors in bis life.
Heere take it hence, and thou for thy reward
Shalt be immediately created Knight.
Kneele downe my friend, and tell me what's thy name ?

Eyden. Alexander Eyden, if it pleafe your Grace,
A poore Efquire of Kent.

King. Then rife vp *Alexander Eyden,* Knight,
And for thy maintenance, I freely giue
A thoufand markes a yeare to maintaine thee,
Befide the firme reward that was proclaim'd,
For thofe that could performe this worthy acte,
And thou fhalt waite vpon the perfon of the King.

Eyden. I humbly thanke your grace, and I no longer liue,
Then I proue iuft and loyall to my King,

Exit.
Enter

Yorke and Lancaster.

Enter the Queene with the Duke of Somerset.

*King.*O Buckingham,see where Somerset comes,   † 83
Bid him go hide himselfe till *Yorke* be gone.   †
    *Queen.*He shall not hide himselfe for feare of *Yorke,*   † 85
But beard and braue him proudly to his face.   †
    *Yorke.*Who's that,proud Somerset at liberty ?   † 87
Base fearefull *Henry* that thus dishonor'st me,   *
By heauen,thou shalt not gouerne ouer me :   † 94
I cannot brooke that Traitors presence here,   † 95
Nor will I subiect be to such a King,   † 93
That knowes not how to gouerne nor to rule,   † 94
Resigne thy Crowne proud Lancaster to me,   † 96
That thou vsurped hast so long by force,   *
For now is *Yorke* resolu'd to claime his owne,   *
And rise aloft into faire Englands Throne.   *
    *Somer.*Proud traitor,I arest thee on high treason,   † 106-7
Against thy soueraigne Lord,yeeld thee false *Yorke,*   † 107
For heere I sweare thou shalt vnto the Tower,   *
For these proud words which thou hast giuen the King.   *
    *King.*Thou art deceiu'd,my sonnes shall be my baile,   † 111
And send thee there in despight of him.   *
Hoe,where are you boyes ?   *
    *Queene.*Call *Clifford* hither presently.   † 115

Enter the Duke of Yorkes sonnes, Edward the Earle of March, and
crooke-backe Richard at the one doore.with Drum and Soldiers: &
at the other doore, enter Clifford and his sonne, with Drumme and
Soldiours,and Clifford kneeles to Henry,and speakes.
    *Cliff.*Long liue my noble Lord,and soueraigne King.   † 124
    *Yorke.*We thanke thee Clifford.   †
Nay,do not affright vs with thy lookes,   † 126
If thou didst mistake,we pardon thee,kneele againe.   † 128
    *Cliff.*Why,I did no way mistake,this is my King.   † 129
What is he mad ? To bedlam with him.   † 131
    *King.*I,a bedlam franticke humor driues him thus   †
To leule armes against his lawfull King.   †
    *Clif.*Why doth not your grace send him to the Tower ?   † 134

H 2   *Queene.*

Queene. He is arrefted, but will not obey,
His fonnes he faith, fhall be his baile.

Yorke. How fay you boyes, will you not ?

Edward. Yes noble father, if our words will ferue.

Richard. And if our words will not, our fwords fhall.

Yorke. Call hither to the ftake, my two rough Beares.

King. Call *Buckingham*, and bid him arme himfelfe.

Yorke. Call *Buckingham* and all the friends thou haft,
Both thou and they fhall curfe this fatall houre.

Enter at one doore, the Earles of Salisbury and Warwicke; with Drum
and Soldiours. And at the other doore, the Duke of Buckingham,
with Drum and Soldiours.

Cliff. Are thefe thy Beares ? wee'l baite them foone,
Defpight of thee, and all the friends thou haft.

War. You had beft go dreame againe,
To keepe you from the tempeft of the field.

Clif. I am refolu'd to beare a greater ftorme,
Then any thou canft conlure vp to day,
And that ile write vpon thy Burgonet,
Might I but know thee by thy houfhould badge.

War. Now by my fathers age, olde Neuils creft,
The rampant Beare chaind to the ragged ftaffe,
This day ile weare aloft my burgonet,
As on a Mountaine top the Cedar fhowes,
That keepes his leaues in fpight of any ftorme,
Euen to affright thee with the view thereof.

Clif. And from thy burgonet will I rend the beare,
And tread him vnder foote with all contempt,
Defpight the beare-ward that protects him fo.

Yong Clif. And fo renowned Soueraigne to armes,
To quell thefe Traitors and their complices.

Richard. Fie, Charity for fhame, fpeake it not in fpight,
For you fhall fup with Iefus Chrift to night.

Yong Clif. Foule Stigmaticke thou canft not tell.

Rich. No, for if not in heauen, you'l furely fup in hell.

    Exit omnes.   *Alarmes*

Alarmes to the battaile, and then enter the Duke of Somerset and Richard fighting, and Richard kils him vnder the signe of the Castle in S. Albones.

*Rich.*So,Lie thou there,and tumble in thy blood,
What's heere,the signe of the Castle?
Then the Prophesie is come to passe,
For Somerset was fore-warnd of Castles,
The which he alwayes did obserue.
And now behold,vnder a paltry Ale-house signe,
The Castle in S. *Albones,*
Somerset hath made the Wizzard famous by his death.   *Exit.*

Alarmes againe, and enter the Earle of Warwicke alone.

Warwick. Clifford of Cumberland,tis Warwicke cals,
And if thou dost not hide thee from the beare,
Now whilst the angry Trumpets sound alarmes,
And dead mens cries do fill the empty aire :
Clifford I say,come forth and fight with me,
Proud Northerne Lord,Clifford of Cumberland.
Warwicke is hoarse with calling thee to armes.

Clifford speakes within.
Clif.   Warwicke stand still, and view the way that Clifford
hewes with his murthering Curtelax,throgh the fainting troops
to finde thee out.
Warwicke stand still,and stir not till I come.

Enter Torke.
*War.*How now my Lord,what a foote?
Who kild your horse?
*Torke.*The deadly hand of Clifford. Noble Lord,
Fiue horse this day slaine vnder me,
And yet braue Warwicke I remaine aliue,
But I did kill his horse he lou d so well,
The boniest gray that ere was bred in North.
                    Enter

The contention of the two famous Houses,
Enter Clifford, and Warwicke offers to fight with him.

Hold *Warwicke*, and feeke thee out fome other chafe,
My felfe will hunt this Deare to death.

War. Braue Lord, tis for a Crowne thou fights,
Clifford farwell, as I intend to profper well to day,
It grieues my foule to leaue thee vnaffailde.

Exit Warwitke.

Torke. Now Clifford, fince we are fingled heere alone,
Be this the day of doome to one of vs,
For now my heart hath fworne immortall hate
To thee, and all the houfe of *Lancafter.*
Cliffrrd. And heere I ftand, and pitch my foote to thine,
Vowing neuer to ftir, till thou or I be flaine.
For neuer fhall my heart be fafe at reft,
Till I haue fpoild the hatefull houfe of *Torke.*

Alarmes, and they fight, and Torke kils Clifford.

Torke. Now *Lancafter* fit fure, thy finewes fhrinke,
Come fearefull *Henry* grouelling on thy face,
Yeeld vp thy Crowne vnto the Prince of *Torke.*

Exit Torke.

Alarmes, then enter young Clifford alone.

Tong Clifford, Father of Cumberland,
VVhere I may feeke my aged Father forth ?
Oh difmall fight, fee where he breathleffe lies,
All fmeard and weltred in his luke-warme blood,
Ah, aged pillar of all Cumberlands true houfe,
Sweete father, to thy murdred ghoft I fweare
Immortall hate vnto the houfe of *Torke* ,
Nor neuer fhall I fleepe fecure one night,
Till I haue furioufly reuendge thy death,
And left not one of them to breathe on earth.

He takes him vp on his backe.

And thus as old *Ankifes* fonne did beare
His aged father on his manly backe,
And fought with him againft the bloody Greekes,
Euen fo will I. But ftay, heer's one of them,
To whom my foule hath fworne immortall hate.

Enter

Yorke and Lancaster.

Enter Richard, and then Clifford layes downe his father, fightes with him, and Richard flies away againe.

Out crook'd-backe villaine, get thee from my fight,
But I will after thee, and once againe
(When I haue borne my father to his Tent)
Ile try my fortune better with thee yet.

　　　　　　　　　　Exit yong Clifford with his Father.

*Alarmes againe, and then enter three or foure, bearing the Duke
of Buckingham wounded to his Tent.*

Alarmes still, and then enter the King and Queene.

Queene. Away my Lord, and flye to London ſtraight.
Make haſt, for vengeance comes along with them :
Come, ſtand not to expoſtulate, let's go.
King. Come then faire Queene, to London let vs haſt,
And ſummon vp a Parliament with ſpeede,
To ſtop the fury of theſe dyre euents.

　　　　　　　　　　Exit King and Queene.

*Alarmes, and then a flouriſh, and enter the Duke of
Yorke, Edward, and Richard.*

Yorke. How now boyes, fortunate this fight hath bene,
I hope to vs and ours, for Englands good,
And our great honour, that ſo long we loſt,
Whilſt faint-heart Henry did vſurpe our rights.
But did you ſee old Salsbury, ſince we
With bloody minds did buckle with the foe ?
I would not for the loſſe of this right hand,
That ought but well betide that good old man.
　　Rich. My Lord, I ſaw him in the thickeſt throng,
Charging his Lance with his old weary armes,
And thrice I ſaw him beaten from his horſe,
And thrice this hand did ſet him vp againe,
And ſtill he fought with courage gainſt his foes,
The boldeſt ſpirited man that ere mine eyes beheld.

　　　　　　　　　　　　　　Enter

The contention of the two famous Houses,
Enter Salisbury and Warwicke.

Edward. See noble Father, where they both do come,
The onely props vnto the houfe of *Yorke.*

Sal. Well haft thou fought this day, thou valiant Duke,
And thou braue bud of *Yorkes* encreafing houfe,
The fmall remainder of my weary life,
I hold for thee, for with thy warlike arme,
Three times this day thou haft preferu'd my life.

Yorke. VVhat fay you Lords, the King is fled to London?
There as I heere to hold a Parliament.
VVhat faies Lord *Warwicke,* fhall we after them?

War. After them, nay before them if we can :
Now by my faith Lords, t'was a glorious day,
Saint *Albones* battaile wonne by famous *Yorke,*
Shall be eterniz'd in all age to come.
Sound Drums and Trumpets, and to London all,
And more fuch dayes as thefe, to vs befall.

Exit omnes.

FINIS.